I0015076

REALISM AFTER THE INDIVIDUAL

REALISM AFTER

THE INDIVIDUAL

WOMEN,
DESIRE,
AND THE
MODERN
AMERICAN
NOVEL

RAFAEL WALKER

The University of Chicago Press   *Chicago and London*

The University of Chicago Press, Chicago 60637
The University of Chicago Press, Ltd., London
© 2026 by The University of Chicago
All rights reserved. No part of this book may be used or reproduced in any manner whatsoever without written permission, except in the case of brief quotations in critical articles and reviews. For more information, contact the University of Chicago Press, 1427 East 60th Street, Chicago, IL 60637.
Published 2026

35 34 33 32 31 30 29 28 27 26   1 2 3 4 5

ISBN-13: 978-0-226-84505-0 (cloth)
ISBN-13: 978-0-226-84506-7 (paper)
ISBN-13: 978-0-226-84507-4 (ebook)
DOI: https://doi.org/10.7208/chicago/9780226845074.001.0001

Library of Congress Cataloging-in-Publication Data

Names: Walker, Rafael, author.
Title: Realism after the individual : women, desire, and the modern
   American novel / Rafael Walker.
Description: Chicago : The University of Chicago Press, 2026. | Includes
   bibliographical references and index.
Identifiers: LCCN 2025015224 | ISBN 9780226845050 (cloth) | ISBN
   9780226845067 (paperback) | ISBN 9780226845074 (ebook)
Subjects: LCSH: American fiction—20th century—History and criticism. |
   American literature—Women authors—History and criticism.
Classification: LCC PS151 .W34 2026
LC record available at https://lccn.loc.gov/2025015224

Authorized Representative for EU General Product Safety Regulation
(GPSR) queries: **Easy Access System Europe**—Mustamäe tee 50, 10621
Tallinn, Estonia, gpsr.requests@easproject.com
Any other queries: https://press.uchicago.edu/press/contact.html

To my grandmother, Mary Warren,
who loved me first and still loves me best.

CONTENTS

Introduction

Literary realism, despite its many rivals, has dominated the genre of the novel since its ascendancy in the English-speaking world. In light of the novel's historical entwinement with modernity, realism's supremacy makes sense. A mode of representation that creates a fictional world populated by fictional people, both usually meant to correspond with an author's contemporary society, realism has proven extraordinarily well suited to the pace and flux of the post-Enlightenment West, a culture propelled, for better or for worse, by its often-acquisitive belief in perfectibility. In contrast to the greater stability and order of the premodern world, the variability of social reality entailed by modernity furnished writers with a fount of material scarcely less deep or diverse than that from which its nonliterary correlate, the news, drank. The loosening of the strictures of tradition, which relied on a religious basis to fix sectors of the population into classes, created two of the principal conditions for the classical realist novel: the individual and society. The former resulted from the erosion of aristocratic privilege and the consequent unmooring of persons from their histories and families; the latter, from the interclass mixing enabled by this convergence of newly invented individuals. For this reason and others, individualism has been treated as inherent to the realist novel for generations of scholars.

But recently greater numbers of scholars of the English-language novel have come to understand that they had been viewing *all* novels from a blinkered perspective—one circumscribed by British and, to a lesser degree, European conventions. The case of Nancy Armstrong, preeminent among today's theorists of the novel, is illustrative. More than a decade after arguing in *How Novels Think* that novels innately cannot distance themselves from individualism, she, with Leonard Tennenhouse, published a study in which they turned their attention to early-American novels. In so doing, they were forced to admit that these novels simply did not adhere to the British model, including, and perhaps most importantly, its promulgation of individualism. Why? According to Armstrong and Tennenhouse, the United States as a republic was allergic to the concept of property—a concept on which Lockean individualism is predicated—something early Americans viewed as "incorrigibly antisocial" (11). As a result of this fundamental cultural difference, their argument goes, novelists in the early republic developed literary conventions more in line with their philosophical vision and at odds with the property-based conventions of British fiction.

Armstrong and Tennenhouse's study—like Thomas Koenigs's even more recent *Founded in Fiction* (2021)—helps clear the way for efforts to consider the American novel on its own aesthetic terms, and this is most welcome. Their focus on antebellum literature and their great attention to the formal differences of the American novel from the British may, however, inadvertently support a stubborn, if now tacitly held, view of American literature that this study seeks to refute—namely, that literary realism is un-American. For, as pertinent as their claims are for early-American literature, a period that saw virtually no realist writing, those claims create the impression that novels opposed to individualism must perforce abandon most of the trappings of classical realism, such as a coherent narratorial perspective and linear, connected plotting. We are still left with the question, "Can a realist novel, interested as the genre has been thought to be in the relation between the individual and society, be realist *and* jettison individualism?"

"Yes!" exclaim the American novelists at the center of this book, *Realism after the Individual*. They are the generation of novelists that came of age during the decades following the Civil War, one of the most tumultuous periods in American history characterized by massive social, economic, and cultural transformation. Unlike the nation's first generation of realist writers—writers such as William Dean Howells and Henry James, who were well into adulthood by this period, their worldviews formed in a different era—this generation of writers faced a world in transition, standing with one foot on either side of history. Disorienting though this position proved to be, it nonetheless enabled these writers to observe the American scene from a unique vantage, one that put them at variance with a number of the foundational assumptions of previous generations. Among these world-defining assumptions was the belief in liberal individualism, which, for reasons I will detail later, struck many as no more compatible with a more developed, modernized United States than Armstrong and Tennenhouse show it to be with a nascent, agrarian one.

The writers I focus on here are a varied group—varied in region, in gender, in biography, and in canonicity, although they all were acclaimed in their day. Born in the 1850s, Kate Chopin, associated with the Creole South and regionalism, is the oldest writer in this study and so, appropriately, serves as a bridge in this book between the old dispensation and the new. Thanks to her recovery in the 1960s and 1970s, mostly by feminist literary critics, her position in the canon is secure. Equally solid are the reputations of elite New Yorker Edith Wharton, born in the 1860s, and Theodore Dreiser, a son of the Midwest born in the 1870s. The Southern writer Ellen Glasgow—also born in the 1870s and, like Wharton, a winner of the Pulitzer—is still known to literary scholars, though her popularity has declined. But their eminent contemporaries are all but lost to history, most of their work no longer even in print. Robert Grant, Robert Herrick, and Booth Tarkington were all well-respected novelists in their day. They all held prominent positions in their societies as well. Grant, descended from an affluent Boston family, received the first PhD in English ever conferred by Harvard and later became a probate judge. He is best remembered not as a novelist but for his role on the infamous advisory committee that judged the Sacco and Vanzetti trial fair, probably out of prejudice against the immigrant defendants. Born, like Grant, to prominent Bostonians, Robert Herrick was a professor at the University of

Chicago for about three decades and, in his final years, served as government secretary and acting governor of the US Virgin Islands. Booth Tarkington—in addition to being one of only four Americans to win the Pulitzer Prize for Fiction more than once (the other three being Faulkner, Sinclair, and, very recently, Colson Whitehead)—served a term in the legislature of his home state of Indiana. Although I will discuss Grant, Herrick, and Tarkington at length here, I could easily have included David Graham Phillips and Harold Frederic, whose novels are entirely in the vein of second-generation realism and who, though popular in their day, have since been relegated.

It is not unheard of for writers to fall out of favor with following generations, and not even these male writers' extraliterary prominence is enough to warrant handwringing over their current obscurity. But theirs, I am convinced, is no ordinary case, and the consequences of their suppression in literary history have been profound. The fact that they are no longer on our radars—not even on the radars of specialists in American literature—has distorted literary history, leaving better-known writers, such as Dreiser and Wharton, as the lone examples of a literary movement that we haven't been able to understand as such because so many within it are no longer studied. In other words, the writers we know have been misunderstood because they have remained outside their proper literary context. Just how confused we've been becomes clear when we consider that all the canonical writers I have mentioned—Chopin, Wharton, Dreiser, and even Glasgow—have been promiscuously assimilated into naturalist and modernist contexts, no matter, as I will explain later, that most of them explicitly distanced themselves from those movements.

The suppression of this generation of realist writers is inextricable from the suppression of realism in American literature more generally. Because I aim to establish these writers' place in American literary history, it would be helpful first to tell the story of how realism—and, by extension, this generation of writers—fell off the map. It begins with Henry James, whose well-intentioned criticism directed at an American predecessor caromed forward in time and injured the next generation of novelists. In his short, trenchant book *Hawthorne* (1879), James based his criticism on an inference drawn from his forebear's penchant for romances, stories set outside contemporary life and less beholden to the standards of plausibility governing realist fiction. James's examination of Hawthorne led him to the grand conclusion that Americans simply could not write realist novels because their fledgling nation lacked what for him was the novel's sine qua non: society and history. James writes, "The flower of art blooms only where the soil is deep . . . it takes a great deal of history to produce a little literature . . . it needs a complex social machinery to set a writer in motion" (3). In the absence of a storied history and dense society composed of different classes thrown into vexed contact with one another, no nation could produce a novel of much worth, he argued. (This conviction helps explain why James, novelist of novelists, trained his sight on Europe and England in his fiction.)

James set an important precedent in dissociating the fiction of his native country from the English and Continental novel. Although British scholar F. R. Leavis, writing some seventy years later, devoted scarcely a word in *The Great Tradition* to any American writer besides James—who, it's important to note, eventually renounced his US citizenship—pioneering Americanist Richard Chase detected in Leavis's work an aspersion cast on the literary legacy of his country. He returned that volley with a book titled *The American Novel and Its Tradition* (1957). Where does Chase perceive this slight? It is in a rather curious source—namely, Leavis's note explaining why he chose to omit the Brontës from his study, Emily in particular. In one of the most bizarre interpretive moves in literary scholarship predating poststructuralism, Chase imagines Emily Brontë as "an American of New England Calvinist or Southern Presbyterian background" and, in this fanciful transmutation, causes this Englishwoman's exclusion from Leavis's "great tradition" to stand proxy for the exclusion of a cavalcade of male American writers (4). The license that Chase affords himself in sparring with Leavis proved productive, for it aided him mightily in his effort to pinpoint the "originality and 'Americanness'" of the literature that he surveys: It helps reinforce his apodictic yet highly debatable

assertion that "although most of the great American novels are romances, most of the great English novels are not" (xii).

Chase's almost nativistic project generated what has come to be
known in Americanist shorthand as the "romance thesis"—the idea,
in Chase's words, that "since the earliest days the American novel, in
its most original and characteristic form, has worked out its destiny
and defined itself by incorporating an element of romance" (viii). Of
course, no claim so bold as this could possibly weather many sea-
sons unchallenged, and challenged it was, by none more vigorously
than feminist literary critics, who discerned in the romance thesis
an inherent bias against women. (Feminist critics objected that
women were unlikely to write the erudite romances of Hawthorne
and Melville, just as the typical plots of romance—sea voyages and
other kinds of flights from "sivilization"—were incompatible with
women's restricted lives.) Yet, for all the exclusions that have been
imputed to the romance thesis and its allegiance to the lives of white
men, no one has inquired into the consequences of this thesis's reliance on the aesthetics of modernism. Without Chase even men-
tioning modernism, that he is leveraging that movement's cachet
in an effort to redeem American literature is crystal clear: To the
romance, he attributes "rapidity, irony, abstraction, profundity"—
features catalogued in any number of modernist manifestos (x).
Again invoking a quintessentially modernist lexicon, he describes
the American romance as possessing "an assumed freedom from the
ordinary novelistic requirements of verisimilitude, development,
and continuity" (ix) and as being "unstable and fragmentary" (x).
In another study of American literature published around Chase's
that tends to get less play—perhaps because it is less jingoistic and
flamboyant—the Yale critic Charles Feidelson more explicitly makes
the link between the American romance and modernism. Feidelson
outright characterizes American romancers' "symbolistic method
as their title to literary independence," and—careful to offer the ca-
veat that these writers "wrote no masterpieces"—he concludes that
"as symbolists they look forward to one of the most sophisticated
movements in literary history" (4). It takes little straining to see
that the "sophisticated" movement he has in mind is modernism.

These and other accounts of American literary history enshrin-
ing the romance would not go uncontested. The 1980s, for example,

produced some of the most damning and generative responses to the romance thesis from such perceptive feminist critics as Jane Tompkins and Nina Baym. However, while their work persuasively identifies the gender bias underlying these earlier accounts and compels attention to the importance of the woman-dominated genre of sentimental fiction, they leave untouched what might have been the romance thesis's chief implication—namely, not only that romance was American but also that realism was un-American. My observation on this score is not a criticism of feminist critics, especially since their focus was on literature antedating by several decades the rise of realism in the United States. But their staging of a battle between masculine romances and feminine sentimental fiction helped create, however unintentionally, a dyad that further erased realism—a movement, it turned out, hospitable to both sexes—from American literary history.

We now know that the rehabilitation of the romance as a national treasure was more than an aesthetic concern. As Geraldine Murphy argues in "Romancing the Center: Cold War Politics and Classic American Literature," "Romance is itself an aesthetic counterpart to the vital-center liberalism of the first Cold War" (738). Ideologically oriented scholarship connecting the founding Americanists' embrace of the romance with mid-twentieth-century politics has taught us that casting the American romance in the image of high modernism helped midcentury critics fashion a literary tradition that comported with the prevailing politics of the United States at midcentury. It also suggests the value, political and literary, that they would have perceived in making recourse to modernist aesthetics: If modernist aesthetics are the aesthetics du jour, and American romances exemplify these aesthetics, then American romances must be good.

However, this accounts for but a portion of the "cultural work" (to borrow Tompkins's term) that tethering the romances to modernism would perform. If we wish to draw a fuller picture of the situation, we are obliged to consider the way the many permutations of the romance thesis positioned realism. Although literary critics from William Dean Howells to V. L. Parrington viewed literary realism as completely harmonious with American values—principally for what they understood as its compatibility with democracy—exponents of the romance thesis conceded that realism belonged to the English and European traditions and portrayed romance as realism's opposite. The opposition of romance to realism is hardly the invention of midcentury critics (Howells and his contemporaries routinely relied on this dichotomy), but it acquired new significance in their hands. According to the critical predilections of the mid-twentieth-century literary establishment, linking the American romance to modernism not only would elevate American literature but also would make modernism seem more American.

To grasp this point, we need only recall the way that *tradition* is defined by T. S. Eliot, whose ideas formed the basis for much of the work done by this generation of literary critics. In his 1919 essay "Tradition and the Individual Talent," Eliot seeks to conceive of literary history as "a living whole" (1095). In so doing, he asserts, "what happens when a new work of art is created is something that happens simultaneously to all the works of art which preceded it" (1093). For him, to speak of tradition is not simply to talk about how successors follow from predecessors; it is also to talk about how predecessors are altered by their successors. In his remarks on Jane Austen, Leavis provides a good demonstration of how this idea could play out in critical practice:

> She not only makes tradition for those coming after, but her achievement has for us a retroactive effect: as we look back beyond her we see in what goes before, and see because of her, potentialities and significances brought out in such a way that, for us, she creates the tradition we see leading down to her. Her work, like the work of all great creative writers, gives a meaning to the past. (5)

Leavis's observations make it apparent that, at this historical moment, in the wake of Eliot, *tradition* had come to denote a particular literary phenomenon. The title of Chase's book, *The American Novel and Its Tradition*, thus warrants reading further into. For, if the understanding of *tradition* at the time came from Eliot—and I would contend that it did—a conception of the American novel's tradition that led to modernism would be a conception of modernism that, to echo Leavis, "gives a meaning" to the nineteenth-century American romance.

The American romance leads to modernism, and modernism illuminates the American romance: This formulation shows us how the Eliotian idea of tradition could perform double duty for scholars intent on establishing the worth of American art. The purported native tradition of romance gets a boost from being associated with modernist aesthetics, and, even more radically, modernism finds itself inextricably linked to an American context at once produced by and, in bringing out its "potentialities and significances," producing the American romance. In conceding a somewhat tendentious version of Leavis's argument—viz., that the realist novel belongs to the English tradition—the exponents of the romance thesis claimed for themselves what, at the time, would have been considered much bigger game: a kind of patent on modernist aesthetics and, in effect, on modernism itself. The bidirectionality of Eliot's *tradition* seals the American romance and modernism together in a virtually airtight container impenetrable by foreign invaders. The nationalistic implications of such a gambit are obvious: If successful, it would place the United States at the very apex of artistic achievement.

The strategy pursued by these early scholars of American literature, in typical American fashion, intensifies the binary hinted at in Leavis's study, turning it into something downright Manichaean. The extreme terms upon which this schema is predicated could not avoid creating distortions in literary history, as Chase himself seems to have been aware. "Let me note again my general awareness of the difficulty of making accurate judgments about what is specially American in American novels or American culture," Chase writes in a telling qualification, continuing, "Yet without a certain rhetorical boldness ... nothing of interest can be said at all on this score" (xii). I doubt any who read Chase's magisterial analyses would reproach him with being uninteresting, but he is certainly guilty of having helped propagate one of the most misleading propositions in American literary history, one whose influences we still feel keenly. The near-purist terms on which he relies in distinguishing an American tradition from an English one essentially foreclose serious consideration of realist novels written by American authors. Why? Because, in order to keep the line of descent between romance and modernism unadulterated and thereby cast modernism as an American invention, realism must be wholly ceded across the Atlantic. And

this is why, while acknowledging that "in Europe some of the greatest novelists have been practitioners in [the novel of manners],"
Chase pontificates, "in America, with the exception of Henry James,
the novelists of manners are among the writers of second or third
rank"—going on to assert that, for American writers, the novel of
manners is not "in their natural style" (158). (The American authors
among Chase's "second or third rank" include the likes of Edith
Wharton, F. Scott Fitzgerald, and Sinclair Lewis, the first American
to win the Nobel Prize in Literature.) Can we resist wondering if, for
Chase, such an argument would imply that English and Continental
practitioners of modernism were perforce second or third rank,
derivative in just the way that he imagined American novelists of
manners to have been?

———————

It is needless to mention that Chase and his contemporaries did not
succeed in persuading the world once and for all that modernism
was a domestic product; the movement's internationalism is, of
course, now universally acknowledged. I *am* persuaded, however,
that their efforts have helped misrepresent literary history in at
least two important ways: First, these efforts have severely retarded
the study of realist novels produced in this country; second, they
have bequeathed us an exaggerated view of the discontinuities between realist and modernist fiction. The first impediment suggests
itself when we consider the fact that, in the middle of the twentieth
century when scholars of the English realist novel such as Leavis
and Ian Watt were laying the groundwork for its study, scholars of
American literature were in large part busy denying that realism
was even American in the first place. That isn't to say that no Americanist studied realist novels; it's just that most who did produced
thematic studies (Alfred Kazin's *On Native Grounds*, for example,
and Larzer Ziff's *The American 1890s*). I can think of few impactful
studies that approached American realism with the same conviction
of its integrity as a literary movement that foundational studies
of the English novel held toward their subject—or that foundational studies of the American romance held toward theirs—*pace*
the efforts of a handful of Americanists who ventured steps in this

direction.[1] This has meant that the same sliver of American realist writers keeps getting discussed, their once-eminent contemporaries now lost to history.

While the study of American realist fiction was revived after the champions of the romance retired, the generation of scholars focusing on it did little to illuminate its aesthetic features or expand its canon. Working in the 1980s and '90s during the rise of Foucault and New Historicism, the cohort dubbed "the new Americanists" were concerned less with what American literary realism *was* than with what it *did*—what ideologies it abetted, what cultural logics it expressed. A vanguard study in this group, Walter Benn Michael's *The Gold Standard and the Logic of Naturalism* (1987) typifies their indifference toward defining American realism. "I use the term *naturalism* here rather than the more general term *realism*," Michaels explains, "not to help breathe new life into the old debate over what naturalism is and how exactly it is different from realism; indeed, I hope to avoid that debate entirely and, if possible, some of the assumptions that govern it" (26–27). For a literary critic, this is an extraordinary dodge and egregious imprecision, but Michaels got away with it because of the low estimate of realism in American literary history—fully reduced, by this point, to a period designation rather than a literary tradition with distinctive features. Michaels's contemporaries joined him in seeking after American realism's ideological functions rather than its literary identity. Amy Kaplan's 1988 *The Social Construction of American Realism*—its title announcing its ideological orientation—argues that "realism works to ensure that social difference can be ultimately effaced by a vision of common humanity, which mirrors the reader's own commonplace, or everyday life" (21). In her 1997 *Reading for Realism*, Nancy Glazener goes Michaels and Kaplan one better, essentially portraying realism as a Rorschach inkblot: "Realism," she claims, "is something that has to be read for" (3), little more than a mutable construct responsible for "producing and enforcing social hierarchies" (14).

I could go on, but I think my point is clear: The study of American realism as such has been eclipsed by the study of what American realism did. Given how inconducive such an approach would be to expanding the established archive of realist novels, it is no mystery how the more-than-century-old prophecy of William Roscoe

Thayer—that "those who undertake to write about Realism in America will inevitably find themselves dealing with it as though it were [Howells's] private property" (164)—came true.[2] But the writers emerging in the generation after Howells were hardly less committed to the realist project. Although published in the years often ceded to naturalism and modernism (the 1890s through the 1920s),[3] their novels—verisimilar, set in their present day, concerned with depicting characters in their relations to dense social worlds— have all the trappings that we associate with literary realism. We see clear examples of the latter tendency in the authors' care in situating their protagonists within identifiable social contexts, such as Herrick's clarification that his protagonist in *One Woman's Life* "belonged to the class too proud to take charity and too incompetent to earn money" (122); Wharton's that Undine Spragg was "the monstrously perfect result of the system" (*Custom* 127); Glasgow's that her Dorinda was born to "the social strata midway between the lower gentility and the upper class of 'poor white,' a position which encourages the useful rather than the ornamental public virtues" (*Barren Ground* 5).

Moreover, many of their critical statements affirm this allegiance. Glasgow states hers unambiguously. In discussing her efforts to avoid the "evasive idealism" she found in most literary depictions of the South, she explains that she looked to nineteenth-century realism for guidance: "From those explorers of the heart, the true realists," she writes, "I learned also, if I had not already perceived this elementary principle in the canons of art, that a universe of ideas divides the novel bearing a sincere emotion toward life from the novel that depends upon a sterile convention" (*A Certain Measure* 17). In an anonymous 1899 letter to the editor of the *Indianapolis News*, Booth Tarkington, a great admirer of Howells, defended his predecessor's realistic approach and sounded remarkably like him while doing it.[4] Taking up Howells's pet cause against the popular preference for romance and sentimental fiction, Tarkington writes, "But if it is well to be lifted out of the commonplace or to be spurred to higher endeavor, it is also well to be made content with common things by portrayals of life of people who are like our selves and to be made to see the charm and interest of life as most of us live it." Interestingly, though, contra Thayer,

Tarkington observes, "Realism is not all of art nor does Howells represent all of realism" (qtd. in Rowlette 65).

Other writers implied their commitment to realism in the negative by distancing themselves from the more self-consciously experimental literary movements of their day. For instance, Robert Herrick, praising Upton Sinclair, writes, "Taken as a whole his fiction presents a comprehensive view of our unlovely civilization and for that reason alone may well become a chapter in the history of American literature when the efforts of his more aesthetically-minded colleagues have long been forgotten" (qtd. in Nevius 176). The most prolific commenter on the craft of this group, Edith Wharton repeatedly—and savagely—disparaged avant-garde writers, perhaps nowhere more sustainedly than in her 1934 essay "Tendencies in Modern Fiction." There she complains of the "feebler" novelists who "beat their brains out against the blank wall of Naturalism" (171). She deprecated as well the modernists' programmatic assault on the past, captured in Ezra Pound's famous credo, "Make it new": "I believe the initial mistake of most of the younger novelists, especially in England and America, has been the decision that the old forms were incapable of producing new ones" (170).

As hostile as Wharton was toward experimentation merely for its own sake, she did not, as the above quotation implies, believe that writers could not renovate old forms for new conditions. In another essay written in 1934, "Permanent Values in Fiction," Wharton reminds readers approvingly of the "incessant renovation of old types by new creative acts" (176). Wharton's statement perfectly captures the attitude that her generation of realist novelists held toward their writing, as their novels make clear. They take their nineteenth-century literary inheritance from classical realism and adapt that novelistic mode for the particularities of their time and place. The epic economic, demographic, and cultural changes during the period in which these authors came of age, the industrializing years following the end of the Civil War, have been documented extensively, and these shifts have been characterized in many ways—among them, as the onset of a "Gilded Age" (Mark Twain's and Charles Dudley Warner's famous epithet), "the incorporation of America" (the title of Alan Trachtenberg's screed), a transition from a production-based economy to one based on consumption, or a transition from a culture of character to one of personality (Warren Susman's translation of the economic transition into cultural terms). Even as early as 1942, Alfred Kazin was able to discern that the period's historical liminality had a shaping effect on its literature. He writes:

> Our modern literature was rooted in those dark and still little-understood years of the 1880's and 1890's when all America stood suddenly, as it were, between one society and another, one moral order and another, and the sense of impending change became almost oppressive in its vividness. It was rooted in the drift to the new world of factories and cities, with their dissolution of old standards and faiths; in the emergence of the metropolitan culture that was to dominate the literature of the new period; in the Populists who raised their voices against the domineering new plutocracy in the East and gave so much of their bitterness to the literature of protest rising out of the West; in the sense of surprise and shock that led to the crudely expectant Utopian literature of the eighties and nineties, the largest single body of Utopian writing in modern times, and the most transparent in its nostalgia. But above all was it rooted in the need to learn what the reality of life was in the modern era. (1–2)

The writers I examine in this study all arrived at the point—whether they began there or not—where nostalgia came to seem a wholly inadequate response to the new world order before them. Glasgow's comment about avoiding the "evasive idealism" of her Southern forerunners—infamous for their nostalgia for "the good old days"—is exemplary in this regard. But the embrace of realist repudiation of nostalgia, idealism, and utopianism are only the tip of the iceberg.

This generation's commitment to describing faithfully their altered world led them to an array of astonishing revelations, but I can think of none more consequential for the novel as a form than the obsolescence of individualism in American society. To be clear, I am not suggesting that, in the era that gave birth to consumerism and therapeutic culture, Americans were less self-absorbed. I am also not referring to the kind of rugged individualism characteristic of the Jacksonian era or discernible in the wolfish acquisitiveness of the corporate magnates (Morgan, Carnegie, etc.—types whose excesses are directly opposed to the moderating, socializing effects of liberal individualism). I am referring to the decline of a particular philosophical paradigm for understanding selfhood prevalent in the West—and especially England—virtually since the dawn of modernity. Elaborated most extensively by the seventeenth-century English philosopher John Locke (and refined most extensively by Immanuel Kant), individualism imagines the human race as a collection of discrete humans—"persons," as Galen Strawson shows in *Locke on Personal Identity*—possessed of autonomous minds and enclosed interiorities impermeable by outside contaminants that they do not voluntarily admit. The individual may be part of a collective—usually "society"—but is not reducible to that collective and cannot, in other words, be conflated with or completely subsumed under that larger entity. The individual's thoughts and feelings are imagined as arising entirely from within that person's mind and body, and, unlike contagion, these thoughts and feelings can never be transferred to another individual without the intercession of that individual's faculty of judgment. As the eighteenth-century refinements of individualism make clear, however, it was not, in the main current of thought, considered an antisocial or anarchical force. On the contrary, writers as different from each other as Kant and Mary Wollstonecraft understood the autonomy one developed through the careful application of reason to have a socializing effect. If, as Wollstonecraft asserts axiomatically, "every being may become virtuous by the exercise of its own reason," we have every reason to assume that she imagines such better beings as aggregating as a better society (129). This explains the somewhat paradoxical description of individualism in Franco Moretti's study of the Bildungsroman:

> Thus it is not sufficient for modern bourgeois society simply to subdue the drives that oppose the standards of "normality." It is also necessary that, as a "free individual," not as a fearful subject but as a convinced citizen, one perceives the social norms as *one's own*. One must *internalize* them and fuse external compulsion and internal impulses into a new unity until the former is no longer distinguishable from the latter. (*Way of the World* 16; emphasis Moretti's)

Individualism, in its ideal form, was not thought synonymous with selfishness; it was regarded as the necessary prerequisite for sociality par excellence (shades of Emerson's riddle, "There must be very two, before there can be very one" ["Friendship" 350]).

Here is an opportune moment to explain briefly why I use the terms *liberal individualism* and *classical liberalism* interchangeably. This is a common practice in novel studies because the two ideas were mutually constitutive, one thought impossible without the other. So close was this conjunction that, by the middle of the nineteenth century, as Elaine Hadley demonstrates in *Living Liberalism*, the liberal individual came to embody the features of the liberal state: Liberalism "uniformly relocates the generative site of rationality from the highly idealized public sphere of collaboration, debate, and circulation to an equally idealized private site of cognition, mental deliberation, and devil's advocacy" (50). And the liberal state came to resemble the individual: "The 'idea of the state' comes to seem like the state as an idea and then, implicitly, the state 'behaving like' the autonomous liberal subject who has ideas" (29).

For generations of literary scholarship, the history of individualism has been understood as coextensive with that of the novel. This link was first clinched in Ian Watt's 1957 *The Rise of the Novel*, in which he located the origins of the novel in the welter of three key emergences—empiricism, individualism, and capitalism, a nexus of mutually reinforcing cultural phenomena. Distinguishing the novel from its antiquity-obsessed literary precursors, Watt claimed, "This literary traditionalism was first and most fully challenged by the novel, whose primary criterion was truth to individual experience— individual experience which is always unique and therefore new" (13). While Watt's explanation of the novel's concern with individual experience links individualism with empiricism, in his attention to the rise of the middle class—in which the people's merit, rather than their histories and families, determines success—we discern his rationale for linking individualism with capitalism. To be sure, there have been notable challenges to this history: Margaret Anne Doody's 1997 *The True Story of the Novel* objects to the Western-centric bias of just about every preceding history of the novel; David Kurnick's 2012 *Empty Houses: Theatrical Failure and the Novel* refutes the idea that the realist novel is invested in inwardness. But these dissents, formidable though they are, have not been enough to dislodge the premise that individualism is central to the realist novel. How else could Armstrong's book *How Novels Think* have gotten away with what it did? Not only does she argue there that novels published in a very specific cultural context—England in the eighteenth and nineteenth centuries—uphold individualism; she takes it a colossal step further, asserting with breathtaking self-assurance that "new varieties of novel cannot help taking up the project of universalizing the individual subject. That, simply put, is what novels do" (10).

As the novelists studied here show, this is not true (and not even Armstrong could maintain this view once she trained her sights on American literature). But, before demonstrating how these novelists dislodged individualism from the novel—as is the aim of the book's ensuing chapters—I need to explain why they did so. Although historians, literary or otherwise, do not discuss it much, one of the main currents of thought near the turn of the twentieth century sprang from a growing conviction that individualism was no longer compatible with American life, and that current was fueled by an ambition to find more apt modalities of selfhood. One could hear the death knell for individualism sounding in various sectors of contemporary culture. In business, John Rockefeller declared, "The day of combination is here to stay. Individualism has gone, never to return," referring to the turn in business toward incorporation and away from smaller-scale, single-proprietor mercantilism (qtd. in Trachtenberg 86). Prominent economist Henry Carter Adams wrote in 1896 of "the regress of self-sufficiency and the progress of association" (qtd. in Livingston, "War and the Intellectuals" 438). In education, John Dewey was trying to reform the classroom to accommodate his anti-individualist view of the self as permeable. According to Dewey, "Bare reference to the imitativeness of human nature is enough to suggest how profoundly the mental habits of others affect the attitude of the one being trained" (333), and he complains later that "the tendency to conceive of thought as an isolated faculty has often blinded teachers to the fact that this influence is just as real and pervasive in intellectual concerns" (334).

Dewey was one of several members of the pragmatist school trying to get beyond individualism. None did so more systematically than George Herbert Mead, whose symbolic interactionalism and idea of "the social self" (detailed in chapter 2) paved the way toward a conception of selfhood in opposition to the self-enclosed, autonomous model presumed by individualism. Mead transforms subject-making from the rational, autonomous, closure-oriented process that individualism posits into an open-ended drama of endless becoming dictated uncontrollably by the social world. In these compulsive acts of social mimicry, there is no intercession of the individual's faculty of judgment, only instinctive, contagious social adaptation. Seeing in the pragmatists' nonindividualist descriptions of selfhood "the solvent of modern subjectivity" (i.e., individualism) (*Pragmatism* 20), historian James Livingston links the decline of individualism in American culture to the rise of consumer culture, corporate capitalism, and associationalism (which entailed, he argues, quoting Gramsci, "'the dispersal of power' from state to society" [9–10]). According to Livingston, pragmatists, like feminists, "understood that the 'progress of association,' and thus the reconstruction of subjectivity, were being driven by the 'socialization' of modern industry via corporate devices and by the implication of the family in a new universe of 'social organizations'" (10–11). Although not directly concerned with the obsolescence of individualism as such, Warren Susman, writing nearly twenty years before Livingston, credits the shift toward a consumer culture with the changes in how people understood selfhood. For Susman, as I explain at length in chapter 2, the shift from an economy based on production to one based on consumption entailed a transition from a culture governed by "character" (a modality rooted in such individualistic values as duty and industriousness) to one governed by "personality" (a much more dynamic modality with striking affinities to Mead's social self).

The rise of consumer culture did more than prompt new ways of conceiving the self. It also determined the demographic that writers—especially the generation of novelists studied here— landed on to help them contemplate new, nonindividualist modes of selfhood. It has been well established that women came to be figured as the exemplary subjects of consumer culture. In *The Gender of Modernity*, for example, Rita Felski explains, "Women's emotionality, passivity, and susceptibility to persuasion render them ideal subjects of an ideology of consumption that pervades a society predicated on the commercialization of pleasure" (62). The transformation of middle-class white women into the ideal consumers (a stereotype still alive today) had many consequences, chief among them the reimagining of women's desire. Once considered constitutionally desire-deficient—"angels in the house" whose desires evaporated upon marriage—women were reenvisioned as insatiable. Middle-class white women were, as Stephanie Foote felicitously puts it, "the targets of a marketing industry that tried to induce in them both the desire to be individuals as well as the desire to be like others" (160)—a formulation that conjures the oscillatory, paradoxical nature of Mead's social self. In Richard Ohmann's *Selling Culture*—a study of the role played by magazines in the formation of mass culture—he details the publishing industry's great challenge in dealing with what seemed an undeniable fact—that, as the primary consumers, women no longer could be understood "as homebound angels softly guarding a haven from the heartless marketplace" (271). According to Ohmann,

> All the magazines labored uneasily with the received idea of the feminine. All felt free to constitute or allude to it as a puzzle, a difficulty, a subject. The masculine posed no such challenge and was almost never addressed, even in [the *Ladies' Home*] *Journal* articles giving advice to young men or to male lovers. The existence of the masculine as "unmarked" pole in the opposition of the genders is of course a very old story, but strikingly retold in this moment of the New Woman. It was women's essence that the new circumstances had thrown into doubt, and that had to be arduously reshaped and patrolled. The principle of unvexed social space could not override that need, because the white, PMC [professional-managerial class] woman's place was a critical dimension of that space. (272)

Furthermore, the seismic shifts in women's lives at the time made them, for many, the perfect vehicles for contemplating a period of American modernity whose future seemed deeply uncertain. According to Jennifer Fleissner—who links the well-known hyper-descriptiveness of naturalism-era fiction to this uncertainty—"If we recognized ... that naturalism's stuckness in place gets linked to the figure of the modern woman, the sense becomes more one of a temporal *suspension*, a deferral of history's meanings by a sense that they will be decided by an unknown future" (*Women, Compulsion, Modernity* 11).

This reimagining of the self largely through reconceiving human desire that I trace in novels of this period took a particular demographic as its canvas: middle-class white women. There is a reason for this. The mostly Northern audience to which the majority of these novels were directed hadn't given much thought to assimilating nonwhite, especially black, people into their conceptions of modernity. Comparing the magazines' reimagining of women to their stagnant treatment of black people, Ohmann observes, "No such urgency pressed upon editors the adjudication of racial essences, for the great northward migration of black people and their visibility as consumers were still in the future, along with the rise of the New Negro" (272). What's more, the kind of excessive desire imputed to white women at this time ran contrary to the aims of black uplift: Having for centuries been stereotyped as hypersexual primitives, black women were pushed toward more Victorian styles of womanhood, their bodies conscripted into the service of the race.

However, although the phenomenon that I describe was overwhelmingly white, race still matters. This way of defining white women through their capacity for desire helped distinguish one form of femininity from its more explicitly racialized other. Moreover, although the discourse of the social self found its way into American literature primarily through depictions of middle-class white women, this trend in fiction was so pervasive at the time that authors writing about other demographics, even nonwhite ones, borrowed techniques from this tradition. In fact, I have argued precisely this in respect of James Weldon Johnson's 1912 novel *The Autobiography of an Ex-Colored Man* (which, interestingly, Johnson had initially intended to title *The Chameleon*, a title apt for many of the novels considered in this study). Focusing on a biracial man who ultimately opts to live as white, this novel, in its attempt to feminize its protagonist, I argue, draws on "the intensely feminized discourse of 'personality' that shaped so much writing in the period his novel first appeared" (Walker 392). This is yet another indication of the influence of second-generation realist writers, whose pathbreaking attempts to reimagine white women through reconfiguring their desire would inspire authors in later years as they turned their attention to new demographics for whom mass culture would entail different implications.

These factors of the second-generation realist novel—its reimagining of women and their desire in consumer culture and their sense that modernity's uncertain future was bound up with women's— helped make middle-class white women appear the most apt figures for rethinking selfhood. They also illuminate two of the most distinguishing features of second-generation American realism, features that it shares with the modernist novel. The first feature is the foregrounding of nonautonomous, permeable versions of selfhood, which means that these writers were already engaged in the deconstruction of the self so often connected with modernism's techniques of fragmentation. For example, consider the modernist method of stream-of-consciousness (a term coined by pragmatist William James, as it happens). In adopting a tactic depicting the mind not as unitary but as contradictory and contingent, modernist writers only intensify the instability of selfhood implied by the ever-mutable selves at the heart of early-twentieth-century realist novels. One of the most salient ways that realist novelists fragment their characters is by curtailing their agency, making it impossible to tell where the world's desire ends and theirs begins. Fleissner captures something very like this paradoxical kind of agency in her useful term "compulsion," which, she explains, "has the potential to name an understanding of agency in which individual will and its subjection to rationalizing 'forces' appear as more deeply intertwined" (*Women, Compulsion, Modernity* 9). As these writers show, however, this kind of agency needn't be seen as peculiarly a literary feature of narrative-phobic naturalist fiction, fiction Fleissner characterizes as being "stuck in place" for its hyper-descriptiveness. In these realist novels, compulsive desire propels plots so inexorably narrative that they appear to continue beyond their final pages.

And that brings me to the second feature they share with modernist art: the "appearance of being unfinished or incomplete" (Lewis 8). In giving plots to protagonists imagined as interminably mutable—because insatiable—many of these writers were compelled to dispense with narrative closure, departing from any sense of an ending. The fact that these novels contain plots that focus largely on courtship and yet forgo closure has obvious ideological implications. To get rid of closure in such a context is, of course, to challenge one of the nineteenth century's dearest institutions and one that the novel has traditionally been instrumental to upholding: the nuclear family. As the first narrative literary movement to abjure closure self-consciously, second-generation American realism is the first *movement* in fiction to subordinate domesticity in the lives of women, the site of what Lee Edelman and others describe as "reproductive futurism." According to Edelman, "Whatever refuses this mandate by which our political institutions compel the collective reproduction of the Child must appear as a threat not only to the organization of a given social order but also, and far more ominously, to social order as such, insofar as it threatens the logic of futurism on which meaning always depends" (11). Although one of my authors, as I discuss in chapter 3, registers awareness of the queerness latent in his depiction of his insatiable heroine (in fact, he puts her in what's hard not to see as a lesbian relationship), it would be a stretch to call them queer. But Edelman's focus on the narrativeness of heteronormative politics—which maintains the child and an optimistic futurity as its telos—helps suggest how subversive these writers were in their rejection of closure. (Indeed, this book takes its alternative to liberal individualism from pragmatism, a philosophical movement contemporaneous with the novels considered here. But, although I do not draw much from, say, queer theory, Marxism, Lacanian psychoanalysis, affect theory, or ecocriticism for models of sociality beyond the isolated individual, the pragmatist model of selfhood—which has received less attention from literary critics than those others—is robust enough to anticipate these later cognate models.)

The open-endedness of the second-generation realist novel seems historically overdetermined. On the one hand, such open-endedness likely worked hand in hand with the culture-wide uncertainty about the future that Fleissner links to the uncertainty of women's future. On the other, it seems only the logical outcome of depicting the life of the ideal subject of consumer culture. Rachel Bowlby conveys a sense of how consumer culture invites endless subjective transformations, finding its most apt metaphor a shop window. Bowlby describes that figure as "a narcissistic mirror . . . which reflects an idealized image of the woman (or man) who stands before it, in the form of the model she could buy or become" (32). While, for reasons I explain later, I reject Bowlby's characterization of consumer culture as "narcissistic," her account helps us see how a culture that positively courted desire contributes to a view of the self as ceaselessly in flux and therefore inherently incompatible with narrative closure. If nineteenth-century realist narratives end when the protagonist gets what she wants (or should want) or simply fails, what happens, these novels ask, when what the protagonist wants is a perpetually moving target? As chapter 3 demonstrates, this generation's renunciation of closure had special implications for the Bildungsroman, traditionally the most teleological subgenre of the realist novel.

A few other scholars have noticed what I am observing about the relationship between realism and modernism—what Brad Evans characterizes aptly as "the peculiarity of the tendency to continue formulating American realism as *against* the modern" (143). Indeed, as he points out, if American modernity is understood as beginning with "the industrializing moment of the long nineteenth century, the modern, then, might be said to correspond neatly with any number of different literary and artistic movements, including the age of realism and naturalism" (140). Fredric Jameson is even more emphatic about how their shared dependence on modernity makes realism and modernism difficult to disentangle from each other, tracing this relationship all the way back to the origins of modernity in the West. He writes: "Genuine realism, taken at the moment of its emergence, is a discovery process, which, with its emphasis on the new and the hitherto unreported, unrepresented, and unseen, and its notorious subversion of inherited ideas and genres (the *Quijote!*), is in fact itself a kind of modernism, if not the latter's first form" ("Antinomies" 476).

Both Evans and Jameson are entirely right in calling attention to the conceptual overlap of realism and modernism. I am in turn calling attention to the *literary* overlap (in both form and content) between the two, an overlap that emerges at the very moment when one has been thought to be on the verge of yielding to the other. When we stop insisting on the antagonism between realism and modernism, it becomes obvious that we should detect in the recognizably realist writing historically closest to modernist fiction all the labor pangs that would produce it. Paul Stasi's distinction between the nineteenth-century novel and the modernist novel is useful for clarifying how second-generation realists bridge the gap between the two literary periods. In *The Persistence of Realism in Modernist Fiction*—a book to which I am obviously very sympathetic—Stasi posits the difference between the two as "one of direction" (22). He elaborates: "Realist novels move their excessive heroes or heroines in the direction of the social. This is the explicit aim of realism's form and of its content—hence the pull towards resolution characteristic of the Victorian novel. Modernist novels, on the other hand, begin with characters who feel themselves to be all-too-painfully social; their most typical gesture is to give voice to a longing to transcend a social world they nevertheless view as inescapable" (22–23). Most of the protagonists of second-generation American realism are indeed pulled in the direction of the social, but, in the prismatic world of the early-twentieth-century United States, that social is inexhaustibly variable. The result is that they are ceaselessly pulled in various directions, "wisps in the wind" (one of Dreiser's dearest metaphors) blown from one social position to another, never fully settling into any. Meanwhile, their insatiability links them to the alienated modernist characters whom Stasi describes above. As is true of the archetypical modernist character, the perpetual longing of protagonists of second-generation realism is pointless, for they will never be happy, are *incapable* of being so. The main difference is that, for better or for worse, they never discover the futility of their quests. Such dark self-awareness would be left for the fiction of the next generation of writers, the modernists.[5]

The question of how modernist writers handle the doomed desires of their protagonists has animated recent monographs in modernist studies, including Lisa Mendelman's *Modern Sentimentalism* (2019) and Pardis Dabashi's *Losing the Plot* (2023). They help illuminate yet another way that second-generation American realists can be viewed as the intermediary between the nineteenth-century novel and its petulant modernist grandchild. Nineteenth-century novels, in the main, end either when their characters achieve what they're supposed to want and thrive or when they embark on a path socially disdained and fail, dying physically or socially. Modernist novels, on the other hand—written at a time when the values of a previous age had been all but rejected—depict a fallen world, where the best that people can do is to recognize what they thought they wanted as the product of false consciousness, that the promises of a former generation are all illusory. The female protagonists in Mendelman's study, for example, "frequently maintain classic sentimental ambitions (e.g., uncomplicated love, felt simplicity, enduring satisfaction), but they consistently come to recognize these ideals as fictions" (3). The protagonists in Dabashi's study, by contrast, fail precisely because they persist in desiring the repressive and retrograde, clinging to a desire for closed-ended plots completely out of keeping with the realities of modern life and that, in many cases, were not designed to serve them well in the first place. Enter the novelists of second-generation realism. Connecting these two recognized literary moments—nineteenth-century realism and literary modernism—is, I argue, a corpus of novels that mostly embraces the insatiability built into modern life but without the distance from its nineteenth-century past required for the self-conscious irony and ambivalence that are modernism's hallmarks. In this sense, second-generation realism may be said to be even more open-ended than modernism—most of its protagonists denied any final lessons, denied even the closure of disappointment.

Dabashi argues also that the modernist novel's "central concern is actually to show that the powers of 'delimitation' internal to the formal structures of Aristotelian fictional rationality—which include action, but also events, locations, characters, and so on—are no longer available after the advent of the modern, social-scientific understanding of human life as a historical sequence of factual occurrences bent not toward narrative intelligibility but toward infinite succession" (19). What she is getting at is that the modernists—the generation of writers immediately following the one I am concerned with—backed away from plotting, particularly from closed-ended plotting, precisely because modern life seemed so utterly unbounded. Second-generation realists paved the way for them by demonstrating how to write about the unbounded subject—a subject without which consumer culture simply could not flourish. Modernist fiction, then, is less a break from realism than an intensification of its later phase. Modernist writers extend their forebears' rejection of closure—their diachronic expansion—to a synchronic expansion that further undermines "plot's constitutively exclusionary work in the nineteenth-century novel" (Dabashi 18). (Think of the profusion of details in modernist fiction; one of Dabashi's shining example is *Ulysses*, in which Joyce seems to include everything, even "bathrooms and the things we do in them" [19].)

In arguing that second-generation realism ought to be regarded as the link between nineteenth-century and modernist novels, I am aware that I'm painting a heretical picture of American literary history. It's long been common wisdom that naturalism occupies this niche. I will confess outright that I believe that the relevance of naturalism in American literary history—and perhaps in literary history in general—has been exaggerated. Not only, as I mention above, did writers of the era explicitly distance themselves from the movement; even its primary proponent, Émile Zola, admitted that he was using the naturalist designation as little more than a branding tool.[6] The insistence of certain turn-of-the-twentieth-century Americanists has led to all kinds of contortions. In some of these contortions, scholars end up inadvertently undermining the distinctiveness of the movement that they are arguing for. Take, for example, the emphasis on determinism in discussions of naturalist fiction. Of course, we know that classical realism was always, to some extent, deterministic—or at least needed to be made to appear so, its ending seeming earned, the product of social laws. (When its endings seemed unearned, novels were liable to the charge of being "romantic," as James called his ending of *The American* [see chapter 4].) Could Isabel Archer have done otherwise than stay with Gilbert Osmond and still remain his "portrait of a lady"? James doesn't have to specify whether she stays or goes because he has engineered the plot in such a way as to make that conclusion foregone, the irresistible fate of the character so circumstanced.

Much as my description of *Portrait of a Lady* sounds naturalistic, many would argue that capitulations to social, rather than, say, biological, laws are acts of moral choice, not rank determinism. But that's just class bias. If, as Eric Carl Link has argued, "it is *theme*, rather than genre, methodology, convention, tone, or philosophy, that qualifies a text for inclusion in the 'school' of American *literary* naturalism" (18), that unifying theme must be, in the main, the plight of the urban lower class. For such a class, fates would be driven by what Maslow has taught us to view as more basic needs: not self-realization (which resides at the top of his pyramid) but food and other creature necessities. This seems self-evident but bears spelling out here: The extent to which one's life is permitted to be determined by higher-order concerns is directly in proportion to one's freedom from lower-order needs. The determinism we see in much of what is called naturalism is only the working-class equivalent of that which we find in more middle-class–focused realism.

At last, naturalism may be little more than realism for the poor, but, although I indicate in chapter 4 the difference between the nation's only card-carrying naturalist (Frank Norris) and his contemporaries, the goal of the book is not to discredit naturalism. I don't wish to deny that the features attributed to naturalist fiction were influences on the modernist novel. For example, there is no question that, like second-generation realism, naturalism dispenses with the autonomous individual, emphasizing diminished agency in the face of environmental pressures (be they from nature or the built world). Fiction called naturalist does indeed, as Lee Clark Mitchell writes, "compel a larger reconsideration of the assumptions we hold about the coherent self" (xii). The second-generation realist novel, as I am claiming, does what realism has always done: It shows characters wrestling principally with their *social* context rather than the mostly impersonal forces upon which naturalism is fixated. My book seeks to identify the defining features of second-generation realism in contradistinction to both its realist precursor and naturalism in an effort to demonstrate the significant role it has played in our literary history. Whereas classical realism treats the social world as influential on its characters' destinies, second-generation realism sees it as decisive. In this later tradition, unlike its predecessor, people don't choose to merge with the social, in the process of legitimation (or consent) that Franco Moretti describes; the social chooses them. And, whereas naturalism maintains the closure of earlier fiction, second-generation realism dispenses with it. For example, naturalism does not, as I show in chapter 4, exhibit the narrative openness characteristic of the modernist plot. In its closure, it is, in fact, less formally experimental than second-generation realism and, in that respect, further from the modernist novel. Indeed, as my treatment of a little-known novel by American literature's arch naturalist, Frank Norris, demonstrates, the closed-ended plots of naturalist novels—notwithstanding all their attention to the seedy dimensions of existence—could be downright conservative. In their open-endedness, the novels I study show that, while the social world has an endlessly shaping effect on their protagonists, determinism and especially fatalism aren't all that applicable here, as they are in other kinds of fiction. Second-generation realist novels are not tele-ological. Put differently, there is determinism in second-generation realism in the sense that characters are shown to be controlled by their social milieux, but the very dynamism and variety of these distinctly modern milieux make that determinism, paradoxically, an ongoing process. Yes, these novels show that the social world shapes people, but that shaping is unceasing, seeming to continue beyond the novels' final pages, which means that this shaping does not lead to some telos, even if its movements are outwardly determined.

In linking second-generation realist novels to modernism, I may appear to be doing just what I accuse midcentury Americanists of— namely, exploiting the cachet of modernism to establish the worth of the texts I study. But I am emphatically not. I am trying, rather, to show how this cohort of writers forms the missing link in the chain of American literary history between nineteenth-century re-alism and modernism. We must remember that, just as these re-alist novels look forward to modernism, they also look backward to nineteenth-century realism. The most recent efforts to under-stand the formal features of the American novel have stressed its differences from its English predecessor. In *Novels in the Time of Democratic Writing*, Armstrong and Tennenhouse invent an en-tirely new critical vocabulary for understanding the early-American novel. In Fleissner's most recent book, *Maladies of the Will* (2022), which is concerned with fiction closer to the period under inves-tigation here, she distances the American novel from the English tradition by attaching it to another. "Typically read for reasons of mere linguistic commonality together with its British counterpart," she writes, "the American novel in fact has arguably more overlap with Continental fiction" (17). While, certainly, I am arguing that the second generation of American realist novelists did something radically different from their English predecessors, I am adamant that they must be understood directly in relation to them. It's true that Fleissner's particular archive—novels foregrounding pathologized, malady-ridden characters—may owe more to Continental writers, but the writers I'm studying respond deliberately to British realism. Fleissner categorizes this latter category of fiction as "an outlier in its more wholehearted resolve to embrace . . . the realist mode" (xi). And this is what makes the American realist novels that I study so striking: They enact a major renovation of their precursor (namely, the nineteenth-century realist novel) and on that precursor's own generic terms. They demonstrate that, even if the romance is the more distinctly American form (as has been maintained from Chase right down through Fleissner), American writers did find in realism a useful resource for expressing the particularities of their place and time.

This in part explains why I employ the concept of individualism rather than something like Fleissner's "will" in thinking about the curtailment of agency in second-generation American realism. For one, I don't think the novelists I examine are primarily concerned with the tension between free will and determinism. In fact, given their formal innovations, it would be nigh impossible for them to be. To think of will is to think, as Fleissner notes, of telos—of design or endpoint (*Maladies* x). One of the signal features of the novels of second-generation realism is the way that they dispense with novelistic closure, an innovation these novelists make in order to underscore the endless flux of the modern subject under consumer culture, a culture that regarded the idea of satisfaction as anathema. Individualism, I contend, is the right lens for thinking about these novelists' intervention because it refers to a specific model of the self with which they were familiar and that their contemporaries in other sectors of culture (primarily philosophy but elsewhere as well) were explicitly impugning. (William James and his fellow pragmatists, for example, were fond of referring to "the old individualism.") Ultimately, though, I see my and Fleissner's books as complementary: Together, they both show how doggedly American authors have interrogated the Enlightenment subject that they inherited, though in different literary modes and therefore through different means.

The self-awareness of the novelists as they pursued their intervention is striking to me. In fact, the punning title of this study—"Realism *after* the Individual"—is an attempt at signaling their remarkable self-consciousness about their adaptations: They are writing novels that come after individualism both chronologically and aggressively. They carefully oppose what they take to be representative—rather than freakish—types from the late-nineteenth and early-twentieth centuries against one another, most often the emergent female social self against an old-fashioned male individual. (When Herrick describes his characters, for example, he mentions, "many hundreds of thousands, men and women, were weaving similar webs" [*One Woman's Life* 69].) The old-fashioned men are consistently killed off in order to underscore their obsolescence in this stage of American modernity and, by contrast, the modernity of the new species of woman. This is one of several features of these novels suggesting that these writers were rejecting individualism—and knew that they were.

In brief, the innovations of this generation of novelists are discernible only against the backdrop of the British tradition—a tradition in which all these writers were far more versed than they were in their native literature. As Wharton notes in *The Writing of Fiction*, "Convention is the first necessity of all art" (54), and British realist novelists set the conventions that these younger American writers manipulate to depict their distinct cultural moment. This is one of the reasons why my method borrows so heavily from "theory of the novel" (or novel studies), a lens, as Michael McKeon explains, uniquely equipped to address the challenge that "each stage in the novel's development purports to evince a radical novelty that simultaneously affirms and denies the coherence of the genre as a whole" (xvi). It is the best method available for conceiving of formal changes as the continuity of a genre rather than as radical rupture—for maintaining a sense of the integrity of the genre while recognizing innovations (and sometimes, as in this case, renovations) occurring as it traverses time and space. Certainly, I would not be able to understand what this generation of novelists had been up to if not for British- and European-centric histories and theories of the novel, and one of the things I hope Americanists take away from this book is the importance of thinking about the American novel in relation to this body of scholarship, no matter that it focuses on different cultural contexts. Conversely, I hope the book shows historians and theorists of the novel the value in taking seriously the American realist novel. At the very least, such a consideration would save them from erroneous generalizations about "the novel" based on culturally and historically circumscribed sample pools. But, more than that, it would aid us in better grasping the impressive variability and resilience of literary realism.

Chapter 1 argues that the literary work of Kate Chopin—and especially her 1899 novel *The Awakening*—should be viewed as a transitional moment in the history of literary realism. Chopin's work demonstrates how the cultural turn to consumerism and self-indulgence radically transformed bourgeois domesticity in America. As much scholarship has shown and as Chopin was keenly aware, this shift helped redirect women's attention from the home to their own personal fulfillment. Yet Chopin did not believe that women would find fulfillment as liberal individualists, historically a male form of self-realization. While experimenting with what we might think of as a romantic version of the self—a self guided by spontaneity and natural pleasures—she ultimately gives us a heroine who stumbles her way into liberal individualism only to find it fundamentally incompatible with womanhood and especially motherhood. In *The Awakening*, Chopin ultimately rejects liberal individualism without presenting a viable alternative for female subjectivity within the possibilities of her era.

But writers following Chopin would do just that. Chapter 2 pairs two of the most eminent exemplars with two of their lesser-known contemporaries: Theodore Dreiser's *Sister Carrie* (1900), Edith Wharton's *The Custom of the Country* (1913), Robert Grant's *Unleavened Bread* (1900), and Robert Herrick's *Together* (1908). A new sort of "social self" emerges in these novels: desirous, other-directed female protagonists who contrast with moribund, self-possessed male characters—the lingering remains of the liberal individual that are symbolically discarded by the novels. The inflexibility of these male characters—their ossified egos—correlates with their outdated faith in the consummation of wedlock. This combination condemns them to failure with their mutable mates. Their old-fashioned views of reality, shaped by a bygone world order, destine them to despondency and death. Their ever-desirous wives, per contra, seem to thrive, outliving their liberal husbands and, in an important sense, the novels that should delimit them. There is little question that these Brahmin authors did not wholeheartedly welcome the changes embodied by their insatiable protagonists. In their unprecedented willingness to depict them and their triumphs, however, these writers show us a modernity where women now appear to be the exemplary subjects—a position from which they had previously been structurally excluded in the West.

Chapter 3 focuses on the shape of the Bildungsroman in this postindividualist age. This genre classically depicts the consolidation of a character's life experiences into a coherent and unique identity, and so it lent itself well to the Victorian association of subjectivity with liberal individualism. Robert Herrick's *One Woman's Life* (1913) and Ellen Glasgow's *Barren Ground* (1925) modify this literary blueprint. The modern subject no longer follows a teleological trajectory ending in either successful socialization or ruin. Herrick and Glasgow therefore leave the reader with little sense of finality. Their avoidance of closure parallels the postindividualist subject's ontological flux, her endless becoming. Herrick's protagonist, Milly Ridge, resembles the social selves of Dreiser and Wharton. Glasgow's Dorinda Oakley, by contrast, exemplifies the philosopher Alasdair MacIntyre's notion of "narrative selfhood"—a communitarian alternative to liberal individualism differing from Mead's social self and tending toward a version of Romantic organicism.

The previous chapters demonstrate how American novelists at the turn of the twentieth century exchange the self-enclosed liberal individual from nineteenth-century fiction for more permeable social selves, using women as the vehicles for this new form of selfhood. Chapter 4 examines whether men could be assimilated into this tradition without being killed off. Excavating the rich archive of American "business novels," this chapter shows the impact of this new mode of characterization on American fiction beyond its portrayals of women protagonists. Noting that many writers of business novels first established themselves through writing about desirous young women, I argue here that contemporary conceptions of the business tycoon, a new figure in the cultural imaginary, were influenced by the nonindividualist forms of subjectivity of this period. In Dreiser's *Trilogy of Desire*, for example, the fearsome moguls of Wall Street turn out to be little more than aggrandized Sister Carries. To reinforce how much writing about women informed these writers' conception of the business tycoon, the chapter turns to another writer of the period, Frank Norris, whose fictional businessmen look nothing like his contemporaries'—largely, I argue, because his heroines do not.

The coda of this book locates the end of this literary tradition in the 1920s, a period in which social mobility and the American Dream were exposed as myths. The novels in this study typically figure the fall of liberal individualism as a war between the sexes—a struggle between a fluid feminine and a rigid male ego, in which feminine flexibility always prevails. The benefits afforded this new subject might appear simply as a female entitlement, as simply what happens to charming, adaptable women such as Dreiser's Carrie Meeber, no matter their socioeconomic provenances. However, Booth Tarkington's *Alice Adams* (1921), emphasizing the difficulty of social mobility in the rapidly stratifying 1920s, presents a flexible female character—virtually identical to those in chapter 2—who ultimately fails to achieve material success or even a good marriage in a novel that perfectly mimics the character of its predecessors but diametrically diverts their plots. Like a laboratory experiment, this novel maintains all other factors constant (womanhood, desirousness, chameleonic social instincts), all in the interest of exploring the determinative effect of class in shaping a woman's prospects in the years leading up to the Great Depression. The coda ends with a glance at how the following generation of writers—the so-called Lost Generation—were influenced by their realist forebears.

CHAPTER ONE

Kate Chopin and the Dilemma of Individualism

In an exquisitely compact piece titled "Emancipation: A Life Fable," Kate Chopin narrates the journey of a beast who has spent his entire life hitherto locked in a cage. Thanks to the "care and protection of an invisible protecting hand," this creature has never wanted for anything: "When he thirsted, water was brought, and when he felt the need of rest, there was provided a bed of straw upon which to lie" (659). This snug existence has satisfied the creature so much that he comes to believe there couldn't possibly be more to the world than what experience has already shown him—that the narrow ray of sun that penetrates into his dwelling "existed but to lighten his home." But everything changes when, one day, the cage's door accidentally swings open (presumably as a result of the owner's carelessness). According to the narrator, the creature is initially quite put out to find the door ajar and would have closed it if not for the fact that "for such a task his limbs were purposeless." Unable to shut himself off from the world outside, he finally pokes his head through the door. However, the immensity of the open sky and wide world prove overwhelming for this being that had never before seen beyond the four walls of his cage.

At least, it does at first. Try as he might, the creature cannot rest with the door open, "for the spell of the Unknown was over him," leading him to venture farther and farther out, for increasingly longer spans of time. Eventually, though, the discovery that there was so much more to see and desire than food, water, and a warm place to sleep overcomes him, and he bolts full-speed out of the cage—"seeing, smelling, touching of all things." Although there are times when he can find nothing to eat, he never returns to his former haven. "So does he live, seeking, finding, joying and suffering." There the short fable ends—in Chopin's characteristically suggestive fashion—with no explanation of why this lowly creature would prefer a life of scarcity to the easy existence he had enjoyed within the iron bars. All we know is that the creature is somehow fundamentally changed through his acquaintance with desire, for "the cage remains forever empty!"

This odd little fable, only a single page long, touches briefly but provocatively on a subject that Chopin would spend much of her short career exploring: the transformative potential of desire, especially for women. Caged and sated, the creature of the fable remains immune to the pangs of desire until his horizons expand, revealing lacks in his life he formerly had no way of knowing existed. The real-life referent of this fable becomes more explicit in Chopin's 1897 short story "A Pair of Silk Stockings," a story almost certainly inspired by Guy de Maupassant's 1884 "The Necklace," also named for a commodity. But whereas Maupassant ridicules his heroine's love for luxury, treating it as ruinously materialistic, Chopin takes the desire of her protagonist seriously, locating in it the potential for self-discovery.

When Chopin's Mrs. Sommers finds herself "the unexpected possessor of fifteen dollars," her actions take a considerable turn away from her characteristically maternal ways. Initially presented as a paragon of maternal self-effacement—earlier that very day, having forgotten to eat because absorbed by domestic chores—Mrs. Sommers at first resolves to spend almost every cent of the fortuitous fifteen dollars on her children: a sturdy pair of shoes for Janie, yards of percale for new shirts for the entire Sommers brood, a beautifully patterned gown for Mag, caps for the boys, sailor hats for the girls. The one personal extravagance Mrs. Sommers permits herself—two pairs of stockings (and these only after she has calculated the costs of her children's new things)—she considers not for her own enjoyment but for her housekeeping efficiency: "What darning [their purchase] would save for a while!" (816).

But the many appeals of the department store bewitch Mrs. Sommers out of her customary asceticism, and her concern quickly shifts away from the children's needs to her own suppressed longings. Thanks to Chopin's richly sensuous language, we proceed step by step through the total seduction of Mrs. Sommers by the marketplace. By the end of her encounter with the silk stockings, Mrs. Sommers is said to have gone on "feeling the soft, sheeny luxurious things—with both hands now, holding them up to see them glisten, and to feel them glide serpent-like through her fingers" (817). When she eventually grows hungry from her busy day of shopping, the mysterious hedonistic "impulse that was guiding her" impels her to take a toothsome lunch of a half dozen bluepoints, a "plump chop," crème frappée, a glass of Rhine, and, as a digestif, a cup of black coffee. "Another time," we are told, "she would have stilled the cravings for food until reaching her own home, where she would have brewed herself a cup of tea and taken a snack of anything that was available" (819). But not on this day. Clearly, the impulse buyer we observe here has come a long way from the self-denying mother who would often get so caught up in ministering to her family's needs that she would forget to eat altogether.

As Mrs. Sommers runs through the fifteen dollars, snatching up every manner of costly apparel and feasting like a queen, her children all but disappear from her thoughts, and, indeed, we hear no more of them beyond the story's first page. Yet, despite Mrs. Sommers's unwonted self-indulgence, the short story terminates on a cable car, in a scene of unmixed longing: "A man with keen eyes, who sat opposite to her, seemed to like the study of her small, pale face. It puzzled him to decipher what he saw there. In truth, he saw nothing—unless he were wizard enough to detect a poignant wish, a powerful longing that the cable car would never stop anywhere, but go on and on with her forever" (820). These cryptic last sentences leave us in a quandary. For one, who is this nonplussed male spectator—nonplussed because not "wizard enough" to detect Mrs. Sommers's desire to prolong her day? Moreover, how do we explain the puzzling fact that, although she has splurged much more than ever before, rather than being surfeited or at least satisfied, she wants more? Paradoxically, Mrs. Sommers's appetite swells as she consumes, defying the commonsensical relation between desire and satisfaction.

The two questions with which this closing passage leaves us— about the significance of the staring stranger and the paradoxical nature of Mrs. Sommers's desire—are linked. Nancy Bentley—in one of the keenest recent analyses of Chopin's work—suggests that the character's "opacity signifies a new kind of interpretive problem" (*Frantic* 145).[1] The fact that Mrs. Sommers, in her altered state, remains so inscrutable to the pensive gentleman is indeed full of metaphorical significance. Chopin's contemporaries believed that the onset of consumer culture created a chasm between the sexes. One reviewer from *The Nation* (clearly more interested in expounding his theory of civilization than reviewing Edith Wharton's novel) reminds his reader of the "inherent difference in faculty between men and women, and an equally apparent difference in adaptability" (rev. of *Custom* 201). "The aspirations for the softer, finer things of life," he continues, "are stronger in the female of the species. The advent of leisure gives more immediate freedom to feelings long repressed." Women were better able to adapt to the nation's rise from scarcity to abundance, he suggests, and, as a result, "we are undoubtedly in the position of having placed woman on a pedestal and left her there lonely and rather dizzy." While their male counterparts maintain the pioneering spirit of their ancestors (only now in the sphere of commerce), women alone have adapted to a new order of self-indulgence, queens among a throng of male drudges.

This reviewer's description of the American woman alone and dizzy on a pedestal aptly characterizes the daydreaming Mrs. Sommers—described at one point as "not thinking at all" (818). In this short story, Chopin, like the reviewer, signals the celerity with which consumer culture was changing prevailing stereotypes of middle-class women, who were imagined to be immersed in the endless pleasures of self-gratification. This metamorphosis was conceived of as occurring so rapidly that it rendered women incomprehensible—almost unrecognizable—to their less adaptive male counterparts. After only a single day of shopping, Mrs. Sommers is made over from the self-abnegating mother of Victorian lore into the self-centered, prodigal woman who mystifies men.

Here consumer culture proves capable of engendering a form of desire that radically alters the presupposed relations between the sexes, transforming middle-class women from the selfless stewards of the private sphere into opaque seekers after self-gratification.

As Bentley observes, "In Chopin self-reflection brings a new awareness of the body, of its immediate sensations and varying states of corporeal consciousness" (*Frantic* 139). In short, Chopin posits the body and its pleasures as sources of revelation just as potent as the mind was understood in classic nineteenth-century realism (including Howells). This feature is on display in virtually all her fiction—from the stories examined above to Chopin's neglected story "An Egyptian Cigarette" (in which a narcotic, usually seen as a vehicle for escapism, compels a woman to confront the realities of her life) and the now much-anthologized story "The Storm," which even Chopin believed too scandalous to try to publish, about a woman who learns the primacy of the body's claims during an infidelity conducted while her husband and son are out at the grocery store.

This emphasis on the body's claims is present even in what is probably Chopin's least esteemed work, her first novel, *At Fault* (1890). A novel taking on—as its title intimates (cf. the legal term "no-fault")—the thorny question of divorce in the nineteenth century, *At Fault* was, unsurprisingly, not popular with editors, and Chopin was forced to self-publish it. Modish prejudices aside, it is not Chopin's strongest work. And how could it be, being as it is among her earliest? It is unsubtle and preachy at moments, its icy protagonist—a young imperious widow—is utterly unlikeable, and it has virtually none of the sensuality of Chopin's masterpieces. If, however, we look carefully enough, we can see even in this early, quasi-Victorian novel Chopin grappling with the effort to reconcile the cogitations of the mind with the needs of the body, especially in the stifled lives of nineteenth-century society women. For, as Donna Campbell astutely notes, "the distinction between realities that have a body and those that exist only in the mind cuts to a central conflict in the book between realism and idealism" (35). The novel ends when the priggish protagonist, Thérèse Lafirme, learns to heed the real laws of attraction above the false ones of social custom and prejudgment, captured in her decision to marry the suitor she had denied in part because he had divorced an alcoholic woman she believed (wrongly) he ought to have supported. The novel's lesson is summed up toward the end, put in the mouth of her suitor: "There is rottenness and evil in the world, masquerading as right and morality—when we learn to know the living spirit from the dead letter" (154). There can be no true morality, the novel suggests, that is not first reconciled with the individual mind *and* body. If Thérèse must listen to her conscience, she must listen to her body too.

Chopin was a great admirer of Walt Whitman, and, like Whitman, she draws on Romanticism's vision of whim, spontaneity, and pleasure as aspects of the self not to be subordinated to bloodless rationality. It is sensual knowledge, I argue, that leads the protagonist of Chopin's magnum opus, *The Awakening* (1899), into what amounts to the birth of an ego, something contemporaries perceived as less developed in women because of their "natural" identification with the home and preoccupation with the needs of others. As we shall see, the birth of Edna's self, facilitated by her immersion in sensuality, assumes the lineaments of selfhood current in the nineteenth century: It is predicated on liberal individualism. As I contend, however, this form of selfhood, perennially only available to white men, proves untenable for a nineteenth-century middle-class wife. Certainly, Edna's failure is meant to be understood as a feminist grievance, as Chopin's way of protesting the limitations on women's lives. At the same time, I understand this failure as Chopin's injunction—in keeping with the associational proclivities of her moment—to move beyond individualism, which wasn't really serving anyone. Edna's sensual awakening leads her to develop the kind of independence at the heart of liberal individualism, but she is forced to the tragic conclusion that this sort of subjectivity, for reasons that will become apparent, is incompatible with nineteenth-century motherhood. In short, while Edna may get a number of things wrong, she isn't wrong, in Chopin's view, to fall asleep on Emerson (605).

The Awakening attempts to elaborate what is only hinted in Chopin's short stories and earlier novel. In what would turn out essentially to be her swan song, Chopin speculates more daringly than ever before on the consequences for middle-class women of society's unleashing of female desire. Although *The Awakening* does not draw the explicit connection between the consumer-oriented market and female desire that we find in "A Pair of Silk Stockings"— set primarily in a shopping center—the novel nonetheless attributes the erosion of the nineteenth-century ideal of womanhood and domesticity to the awakening of female desire. As is true of Mrs. Sommers, the kindling of Edna Pontellier's desire renders her unrecognizable to the other characters of the novel, the male characters especially. The novel begins with Edna's husband, Léonce, complaining that she is "burnt beyond recognition" after indulging in a swim far more pleasing to her than to him—a tipping of the scales that, even at this early point in the plot, puts Edna at variance with standards for femininity. The narrator suggests that it is her violation of convention that upsets her husband and renders her "beyond recognition": "What folly! to bathe at such an hour in such heat," he raves (522). Once more recalling Mrs. Sommers, "beyond recognition" here becomes synonymous with "beyond convention." Later, when Léonce upbraids Edna for neglecting her household duties, the narrator notes that "he could see plainly that she was not herself." But, just when we think that Léonce understands his wife, we are assured of his misrecognition: "That is, he could not see that she was becoming herself and daily casting aside that fictitious self which we assume like a garment with which to appear before the world" (586–87). Her self-indulgence appears to have made her a stranger to the very person who should know her best.

The predominance of the word *self* in this passage and throughout the novel offers an important clue to what the awakening of desire within Edna has done to her. It has aligned her with Mrs. Sommers's "poignant wish . . . that the cable car would never stop anywhere, but go on and on with her forever"—a wish that, if fulfilled, would separate her from her children and from obligation forever. Initially intending to title the novel "A Solitary Soul," Chopin changed it only at her editor's urging. This retitling of the novel, however, distracts from the fact that her heroine's greatest wish is simply to be left alone. Edna and the narrator express this sentiment frequently enough to make it clear: "[The absence of her children] seemed to free her of a responsibility which she had blindly assumed and for which Fate had not fitted her" (541); "Every step which she took toward relieving herself from obligations added to her strength and expansion as an individual" (629); "But I don't want anything but my own way" (650), she insists, and, even more succinctly, "I want to be let alone" (649).

Despite the simplicity of this wish—to be left alone—critics have often understood Edna's longings as fantastical. In agreement with Willa Cather's scathing review of *The Awakening*, for instance, Susan J. Rosowski conflates Edna Pontellier's problem with Emma Bovary's, proposing that her dilemma lies in the fact that "woman must choose between her inner life of romance and the outer world of reality" (54). In a more generous interpretation of the novel, Sandra Gilbert argues that "*The Awakening* is a female fiction that both draws upon and revises *fin de siècle* hedonism to propose a feminist and matriarchal myth of Aphrodite/Venus as an alternative to the masculinist and patriarchal myth of Jesus" (91).[2] According to Gilbert, the novel "shows, from a female point of view, just what would 'really' happen to a mortal, turn-of-the-century woman who tried to claim for herself the erotic freedom and power owned by the classical queen of love" (92).

Interpretations such as these tend to locate Edna's problem in the ether, romanticized and remote, but readers would err to alienate her dilemma from the real world of human relations. Adapting Gilbert's language, we might put the point this way: *The Awakening* shows just what would really happen to a turn-of-the-century mother who tried to claim for herself the privileges of liberal individualism. Liberal individualism, an ideology that framed the way people conceived of the self in the nineteenth century, stresses the autonomy, self-enclosure, and privacy of the individual. For many widely noted reasons, this form of self-realization was, practically, only available to white men.[3] This is what makes Edna's urge so transgressive, for her desire to be left alone amounts to a liberal wish for self-possession.[4] This fact is doubtless at the root of Andrew Delbanco's provocative suggestion that *The Awakening* be read as a "novel of passing"—not "about a light-skinned black passing for white" but about "a woman passing for a man" (104). While Delbanco may be guilty of reading a bit too literally, he is entirely right to suggest that Chopin's frequent masculinization of Edna is hardly accidental.[5] When Chopin notes that Edna has "strong, shapely hands" (in contrast to the other ladies' "dainty and discriminating fingers") (522), that she is "rather handsome than beautiful" (524), that she "drank the liquor from the glass as a man would have done" (612)—when Chopin describes her heroine in these masculine ways, she is metaphorically demonstrating that the liberal privileges of self-possession of which Edna is increasingly trying to avail herself are essentially male privileges. Put differently, to be a liberal individual is, in Chopin's mind, to be a white man.

Even before her transformative swim at Grand Isle—commonly understood as the turning point in the novel—the narrator carefully distinguishes Edna from the "mother-women" around her in order to establish her incongruence with idealized nineteenth-century femininity. Mother-women "idolized their children, worshiped their husbands, and esteemed it a holy privilege to efface themselves as individuals and grow wings as ministering angels" (529). But Edna is simply "fond of her husband," possessing "no trace of passion or excessive and fictitious warmth . . . that might threaten its dissolution," and "fond of her children in an uneven, impulsive way" (541). The consummate mother-woman, Edna's matchlessly feminine friend Adèle Ratignolle, serves to throw Edna's unconventionality into relief. Adèle is feminine to the point of cliché: "There are no words to describe her save the old ones that have served so often to picture the by-gone heroine of romance and the fair lady of our dreams" (529). Significantly, she is customarily cloaked in "a fluffiness of ruffles," which "suited her rich, luxuriant beauty as a greater severity of line could not have done" (536–37). In contrast, Edna is sharply delimited: The "lines of her body were long, clean and symmetrical"; she displays a striking "severity of poise and movement"; her hat "clung close to her head" (536). These casually mentioned details hint at these women's differently constituted ego boundaries, the integrity and autonomy of Edna's self versus Adèle's psychological fluidity and organic oneness with her community. This contrast is brought into view once more when Edna withdraws from the sewing circle one afternoon at Grand Isle, where we find Adèle thriving among her fellow mother-women. Edna abandons this scene of female sociability—a visual representation of the intense bonding that suffuses the idealized "woman's sphere"—in favor of a more solitary, stereotypically more masculine exercise. While these women tranquilly knit away, symbolizing the intertwinement of their lives, Edna extracts herself from the communal web of love and ritual to paint an impressionistic portrait of Adèle.[6]

After her first swim at Grand Isle, Edna's differences from the women around her grow even more explicit. What was merely hinted at before finds clear expression in Edna's bold declarations. For instance, whereas the other women take pride in self-effacement, after the swim, Edna insists on the sanctity of her self. "I would give up the unessential; I would give my money, I would give my life for my children," Edna explains to Adèle, "but I wouldn't give myself" (575). Adèle replies, "I don't know what you would call the essential, or what you mean by the unessential . . . but a woman who would give her life for her children could do no more than that—your Bible tells you so. I'm sure I couldn't do more than that." As the bemused response of this spokeswoman for mother-womanhood suggests, Edna's reference to a metaphysical self irreducible to her life seems nonsense coming from the mouth of a married woman. What more, Adèle asks, does a woman have to give up than her life? In her insistence upon an inalienable self—"I wouldn't give myself"—Edna rehearses one of liberalism's dearest tenets, that individuals have property in their persons.[7] Yet, as a woman of the nineteenth century, Edna is presumed to be the property of her husband, hence the novel's opening passage, in which Léonce eyes his sunburned wife "as one looks at a valuable piece of personal property which has suffered some damage" (522).

But what is it about the swim that so profoundly dissatisfies Edna with being owned? Though readers have perceived the centrality of Edna's sublime attempt to swim "where no woman had swum before," this pivotal moment remains ill understood. Attention is usually reserved for the novel's other important swim, in which Edna ends her life (on which, more later). This scene, however, is likely the novel's most concentrated expression of the feeling animating Edna—of what the narrator obliquely dubs "more wisdom than the Holy Ghost is usually pleased to vouchsafe to any woman" (535). The swim dramatizes the birth of Edna's ego, of consciousness of "her relations as an individual to the world within and about her" (535).

The felicity of swimming as a figure for Edna's awakening into desire for full autonomy lies in the way that submersion in water envelopes the entire body in a uniform sensation, thereby generating a feeling of the body's wholeness. Moreover, the act of swimming places the swimmer's survival completely into her own hands. These are precisely the aspects of Edna's swim on which the novel dwells. "She would not join the groups in their sports and bouts," we are told, "but intoxicated with her newly conquered power, she swam out alone" (552). This brief swim allows Edna to luxuriate in the semiconscious feeling of oneness and self-sufficiency that ultimately prove illusory on land.

Given the deep solipsism of this episode, it is puzzling that so much effort has been spent on trying to designate a person outside of Edna as the inspiration for her awakening. For instance, Kenneth Eble, one of the novel's earliest admirers within the academy, concludes, "Quite frankly, the book is about sex," nominating the novel's men (central among them the craven Robert Lebrun) as the initiators of Edna's awakening (9). Kathleen Margaret Lant dissents from such readers as Eble, arguing for Adèle's influence on Edna. Elaine Showalter likewise asserts the importance of women in Edna's development, adding Mademoiselle Reisz to the mix ("Tradition" 45–46). Yet Chopin seems intent on portraying Edna's awakening as an event entirely internal—as an enthusiastic response to the sea's invitation to "the soul to wander for a spell in abysses of solitude; to lose itself in mazes of inward contemplation" (535). The novel appears to anticipate readers' temptation to attribute Edna's awakening to sources outside herself when, during her swim, it pokes fun at the onlookers who each "congratulated himself that his special teachings had accomplished this desired end" (552). As the construction of the sentence suggests—it easily, and probably more efficiently, could have been constructed in the plural (e.g., "they all congratulated themselves")—Chopin wants us to know that the self-congratulatory onlookers whom the narrator mocks are all men. It is part of her effort to remove all doubt that men—and, by extension, sex—are, at most, incidental to her heroine's transformation.

Immediately after her brief but life-altering dalliance with pure autonomy, Edna's sense of self enlarges to the point of eclipsing her view of the personhood of others. "The people about me," she notes on her way up from the shore, "are like some uncanny half-human beings" (553). At this moment, she is speaking in the register of fantasy, playfully swapping improvised fairy tales with Robert, but the altered view of herself that she expresses here is meant in earnest. Awakened to the great magnitude of her self, she has come to regard the property she possesses in it as too precious to yield to another. This sentiment first manifests itself as a refusal to bend to the will of others, most importantly her husband's. When Léonce returns from the shore, he finds Edna lying awake in a hammock right in front of their Grand Isle house. Notwithstanding his many injunctions to abandon the hammock and join him for bed, Edna resolutely declines, countering his commands with a stiff-necked "Léonce, go to bed" (556). "Another time," the narrator notes, "she would have gone in at his request" (555). This we know to be true, for, only a few nights earlier, she had instinctively obeyed him when, on his late-night return from the men's club, he churlishly demanded that she get up to check on one of the children (though she had been "quite sure Raoul had no fever" [526]). However, as she reflects on such moments while in the hammock, her past responses seem entirely foreign to her: "She could not realize why or how she could have yielded, feeling as she then did" (556).

For an awakened Edna, all externally imposed conventions come to seem deep infringements on her desire for self-determination, and the remainder of the novel—all the way to the very last page— traces her attempt to discard them. After a heated disagreement with her husband over her neglect of "*les convenances*," for instance, Edna retreats to her bedroom to throw a tantrum. Desiring simply to "destroy something," she smashes a vase against the hearth and hurls her wedding ring to the floor, stomping it with the heel of her boot. We are meant to view this frenzied display as Edna's revolt against the institution most threatening to her personal freedom: wedlock. But the outcome of her rebellious paroxysm bodes poorly for her emancipatory enterprise. "Her small boot heel," we learn, "did not make an indenture, not a mark upon the little glittering circlet" (581).

In Edna's ensuing quest for liberation, proprietary issues come to occupy a place of increasing importance in the novel. We have noted already her desire for self-possession—her resolve "never again to belong to another than herself" (613). However, as Delbanco notes, Edna comes to develop a more expansive "taste for ownership" (98). When, for instance, Mademoiselle Reisz asks why she has opted to move out of the Pontellier home and into a dwelling modest enough to merit the name "the Pigeon house," Edna explains, "The house, the money that provides for it, are not mine" (613). Mademoiselle Reisz replies, "They are your husband's," puzzled by Edna's complaint. But Edna clarifies that it is a room wholly her own that she seeks, detailing the independent means that have enabled her to procure the space: "I have a little money of my own from my mother's estate, which my father sends me by driblets. I won a large sum this winter on the races, and I am beginning to sell my sketches. . . . I know I shall like it, like the feeling of freedom and independence" (613).

Had Chopin stopped here, we might well have ended up with the tale of female liberation that much feminist criticism has found in *The Awakening*. But Chopin makes clear that the kind of liberty that Edna seeks—pure autonomy, complete freedom from relation—is impossible. As a few critics have pointed out, Edna's quest for independence is predicated upon dependence. Right before she gushes to Mademoiselle Reisz about the "feeling of freedom and independence" she anticipates in removing to the Pigeon house, for instance, she notes that "Old Celestine," one of the black servants employed in the Pontellier home, "says she will come stay with me and do my work" (613). Elaine Showalter was one of the first critics to point out the illusory nature of Edna's independence: "Floating along in her 'mazes of inward contemplation,' Edna barely notices the silent quadroon nurse who takes care of her children, the little black girl who works the treadles of Madame Lebrun's sewing machine, the laundress who keeps her in frilly white, or the maid who picks up her broken glass. She never makes connections between her lot and theirs" ("Tradition" 51). For Showalter, this is not just Edna's problem but Chopin's as well. Just as Edna "never moves from her own questioning to the larger social statement that is feminism"(51), Chopin, in her "literary solitude" and refusal to situate her work within a "woman's tradition," fails in her novel "to work out something different and new" (48).

Similarly, Michele A. Birnbaum demonstrates the many ways Edna's erotic emancipation depends on appropriation and exploitation. According to Birnbaum, "Edna locates in racial and ethnic

Others a territory necessary for a liberating alterity: in their difference, she finds herself" (303). Although Birnbaum does not as
explicitly conflate Edna and Chopin, the suggestion that they might
share the same blind spot appears in her essay nonetheless, if for no
other reason than that Birnbaum depicts Chopin as the unselfcon-
scious creator of an objectionable heroine. I echo Jennifer Fleissner
in posing to such critics as Showalter and Birnbaum the following
question: If there is no suggestion that Edna sympathizes with the
many women around her, "what should we say of the author who
has brought that dissatisfaction to our attention in the first place?"
(*Women, Compulsion, Modernity* 244).

Fleissner's question is indispensable to any understanding of
the novel, even though she does not pursue it fully. The details in
the narration undermining Edna's claim to unbridled autonomy
are too numerous and too conspicuous to seem unintentional. It
seems more reasonable to assume that both we *and* the author
perceive the gap between Edna's individualistic aspirations and
her reality. As we shall see, the narrator's attempt to belie Edna's
autonomy is significant. First, however, it is important to note the
way in which Edna's quest for freedom hinders her relationships,
alienating her to a point that ultimately proves unbearable. Besides
Edna's unacknowledged reliance upon the labor of her domestic
servants, Chopin portrays all of Edna's relationships as exploitive,
crucial instruments whose importance Edna must ignore in order
to maintain the illusion of her autonomy. In Edna's relationship
with Mademoiselle Reisz, we find the most salient proof that her
exploitive tendencies infect more than just her relations with her
black servants. Edna's disdain for this ostracized spinster is hardly
concealed (548). When, for instance, Mademoiselle Reisz tells Edna,
"I really don't believe you like me," Edna strains at civility, replying,
"I don't know whether I like you or not" (592). Yet Edna continues
her relationship with Mademoiselle Reisz because it is through her
alone that she can nourish her temporary infatuation with Robert,
who writes his most confidential letters to this eccentric woman.
Though Edna may remain unaware of her need to exploit Mademoiselle Reisz, the latter herself is certainly not. When Edna storms
into this woman's home imperiously issuing demands—"Show me
the letter and play for me the Impromptu"—Reisz complies but not

without revealing that she is aware of being used. With a "wriggling laugh," just before she fetches the letter and sets herself to playing the requested composition, she describes herself as "a foolish old woman whom you have captivated" (594).

In her pursuit of freedom, Edna seeks independence and solitude, admitting relations only insofar as they enhance her ability, as she puts it, to "have my own way" (650). As the novel suggests, Edna is not the only woman seeking to have her own way and trying to exceed the limitations of the traditional "woman's sphere." When Léonce first consults Dr. Mandelet about his wife's erratic behavior, the doctor instantly asks, "Has she been associating of late with a circle of pseudo-intellectual women—super-spiritual beings?" (596). Of course, Dr. Mandelet is referring to the many feminist circles of the turn of the century. Interestingly, had those circles been to blame for Edna's puzzling actions, Léonce, as he himself suggests, might have been slightly more at ease: "That's the trouble . . . she hasn't been associating with any one" (596).

The nature of Edna's quest for freedom, centering on freedom from relation—on the achievement of unencumbered autonomy—unfits her not only for friendship (as we see in her exploitive tendencies toward those around her) but also for the collaboration required by feminism and by American culture in general, in its turn to more associational forms (e.g., corporate capitalism).[8] As historian James Livingston explains, many contemporary intellectuals believed that the "'socialization' of modern industry via corporate devices" and "the implication of the family in a new universe of 'social organizations'" were driving American society away from individualistic forms of self-definition and toward more associational forms (*Pragmatism* 11). Examining the attempts of pragmatist philosophers and feminists of the era to understand self-formation in more radically associational terms, Livingston sees in Chopin's nonliterary contemporaries the capacity to "suffer the dissolution of . . . the form of subjectivity specific to the 'era of the ego,' circa 1600–1900" (10). As Livingston's study suggests, for many at the time, individualism had lost its relevance as a model for middle-class life.

However, in the epoch that thinkers extending from Chopin's time to our own have characterized as the age of association, the oddly literalized Emersonian self-reliance that Edna seeks comes to appear not only chimerical but also lethal. Toward the end of the novel, during her final swim, Edna appears to catch a glimpse of the role her self-sequestration has played in her demise, musing, "Perhaps Doctor Mandelet would have understood if she had seen him—but it was too late . . ." (655). Even in the sea—the birthplace of her desire for pure autonomy and the only place where she has felt anything remotely like it—even here, thoughts of relationality and interdependence haunt her, including the relation that has loomed largest throughout the novel. In addition to faint speculations on the difference the doctor might have made, images of family—of her father and sister Margaret—flash before her, culminating in the final "hum of bees, and the musky odor of pinks" that bookend the novel and her life (655). These are symbols of generation and motherhood, and they bring Edna's mind back to the one relation that she could elude only through sacrificing her life—which, we should recall, she groups with the "unessential," in contradistinction to the inviolable metaphysical self that she earlier tries to describe to Adèle Ratignolle. "Remember the children!"—the penetrating admonition that Adèle had voiced to her while in the throes of labor—thrusts before Edna that one unshakable relation, her relation to her children and concomitant responsibility to them. And here we confront the incompatibility of liberal individualism with motherhood: Yes, individualism insists on one's right to be left alone, but it also requires that one not infringe on anyone else. Because of the configuration of nineteenth-century motherhood, Edna's unmotherly behavior would inevitably harm her children, not least in ruining their social standing. "She had said over and over to herself: 'To-day it is Arobin; to-morrow it will be some one else. It makes no difference to me, it doesn't matter about Léonce Pontellier—but Raoul and Étienne!" (653). Through Adèle's indelible reprimand, Edna realizes that preserving what she has grown to regard as the unessential, the property she has in herself, would, in fact, require her death.

Some critics have provocatively argued that we ought not assume that Edna commits suicide, believing such an interpretation too defeatist for a novel so revolutionary.[9] However, these readers have had great difficulty accounting for the hard distinction between the essential and unessential self—the metaphysical (her intellectual and spiritual autonomy) and the physical (her life)—on which Edna insists. When we observe how much of Edna's preparation for the swim involves shedding—of "the unpleasant, pricking garments"—we are prompted to recall that distinction; the discarded bathing suit symbolizes the "unessential" (her life) that she must now sacrifice to preserve the essential. (The metaphor is just too heavy-handed to miss.) Given the limitations on women's lives in the nineteenth century, suicide was practically the only way for Edna to live out liberal individualism, with its commitment to freedom (as opposed to the "soul's slavery" that living has come to represent for her) (654). Therein lies Chopin's quarrel with her era. Though Chopin is indeed disapproving of her heroine's individualistic ways—hence the sometimes unflattering portrayal of Edna—she nonetheless deplores the fact that individualism remained nonviable for women like Edna solely because of their gender, race, and class. At the same time, as Chopin was well aware—in the representation, for example, of husbands and male children—liberal individualism, and all the independence its suggests, was equally fictitious for white men too. They depended on—exploited and appropriated—others exceedingly more than any other demographic.

Still, the problems facing Edna as a woman attempting the path of individualism are distinct. Patricia S. Yaeger helps us see a subtler yet no less powerful way Edna's gender thwarts her. Bringing poststructuralist theory to bear on the novel, Yaeger suggests "*The Awakening*'s most radical awareness is that Edna inhabits a world of limited linguistic possibilities, of limited possibilities for interpreting and re-organizing her feelings, and therefore of limited possibilities for action" (200). Put differently, Edna cannot work out a solution for her dilemma because she lacks the language necessary for even conceiving of what she wants. Hence her vague and convoluted complaints: "But I don't want anything but my own way. That is wanting a good deal, of course, when you have to trample upon the lives, the hearts, the prejudices of others—but no matter—still, I shouldn't want to trample upon the little lives" (650).

Implying that the absence of a speech community is central to Edna's conflict, Yaeger's interpretation of the novel seems right insofar as it highlights Edna's "need for a more passionate and intersubjective speech" (204). However, instead of nominating the language of romance as the idiom that most clouds the heroine's judgment, as Yaeger does, I would suggest the language of liberal individualism. For one, understanding Edna's story in this way prevents the overestimation of Robert Lebrun's importance in the novel that results from such interpretations as Yaeger's and many others'. Love, after all, is but one of multiple avenues through which Edna seeks solitary fulfillment. (We mustn't forget her passion for art and economic independence.) And, perhaps more importantly, it would help us grasp why relation in general—a concern that, in some way or another, links most critical treatments of *The Awakening*—becomes such a crucial problem in the novel.

It is clear that, in writing *The Awakening*, Chopin was seeking a way of imagining women's lives that differed from the prevailing options, embodied by the two enigmatic figures amid whom Edna so often finds herself—the young lovers and the doleful widow in black. Larzer Ziff suggests that these two figures represent "the horizons of experience" (20). He appears to imply the antipodal experiences of bliss and mourning, but I believe that Chopin has in mind the narrow range of experience afforded women in fiction. Though the young lady doting on her suitor and the widow in mourning exist on opposite ends of the continuum of heterosexual love, their lives nonetheless remain tethered to that continuum—one ceaselessly basking in love, the other ceaselessly grieving its loss. However, in Chopin's mind, the turn of the twentieth century opened the door of the stupefying love-cage that had falsely restricted women's desire, much as entrapment initially restricts the freed beast with whom this chapter began.

We see Chopin's exhaustion with the limitations that literary convention had placed on the writing of women's lives in her short story "Miss Witherwell's Mistake." There, Mildred Witherwell is sent to live with her aunt after her father learns of her dalliance with a young man of modest wealth. Her aunt, though a spinster, espouses the most conventional ideas about women and wedlock and even earns a living from writing stories and short tracts upholding all things traditional, including the widespread stereotypes about women (in addition to love stories, treatises titled "Security

Against Moths," "A Word to Mothers," and so forth). It just so happens that the lover Mildred left in St. Louis found employment as
an editor at the very periodical that publishes her aunt's paeans
to the status quo. The two eventually meet and covertly resume
where they left off in St. Louis. Apparently attempting to figure out
her dilemma through writing a story of her own, Mildred consults
her aunt when the story's protagonist reaches, as she herself has,
the point where her desires and convention diverge. "Bear in mind
that being brought—almost forced together—through outside
influences, they grow to love each other to desperation," Mildred
explains (689). Without the slightest hesitation, her aunt replies,
"Your hero must now perform some act to ingratiate himself to the
obdurate parent." When Mildred objects that she "can't force the
situation"—being as she is "extremely realistic"—an "aghast" Miss
Witherwell retorts, "The poison of the realistic school"—the very
school to which Chopin herself belonged—"has certainly tainted
and withered your fancy in the bud, my dear, if you hesitate a moment. Marry them, most certainly, or let them die" (690).

Of course, this scene enables Chopin to enact another of her sig-
nature plot twists—the aunt inadvertently encourages her niece to
violate her father's wishes and marry the impecunious editor—but
I think there is yet more to grasp here. In her orthodox response to
her niece's attempt to imagine new directions for her life, the aunt
closes off potentially fruitful veins of thought—ones that might
lead her niece to discover new modes of artistic expression as well
as new, possibly more fulfilling ways to live. Miss Witherwell's tit-
ular mistake consists not simply in the fact that she sent her niece
to the publishing office unaccompanied or that she accidentally
encouraged her to defy her father's wishes. Her mistake is that she
enabled the conventions of love to falsify a work of art and to detour
a life from what might have been a more salutary course.

Edna, too, might have thrived had she been able to find a viable
third path beyond the dichotomy of love and death endorsed by that
parrot of tradition, the elder Miss Witherwell. Such a path, Chopin
makes clear, would not lead to the embrace of unencumbered individualism—a way of life hardly viable for men in this era (even
Edna's husband makes his living from joint-stock ventures in New
York) and much less so for a mother. It would seem that Edna's task

lay not in the impossible act of ridding herself of relations. It lay in finding some way to reconfigure relatedness—inevitable always but, at this moment in history, undeniable—into a more endurable state of being.

How she might do so Chopin does not say. But what Chopin does make clear is that, though women's desires were beginning to exceed the narrow scope usually afforded them in nineteenth-century fiction, their lives would not conform to the shape of liberal individualism. Indeed, they would not follow the path long imagined for men. Although she does not present a more viable form of female subjectivity in this age of awakened desire, her work constitutes an important step in reimagining women in fiction at a moment when gender relations were rapidly changing in reality. Chopin's untimely death at fifty-four robbed her of the opportunity to continue developing her view of how the changes in American life would affect women and, more generally, prevailing understandings of the self. But, as the next chapter shows, her younger contemporaries would pick up where she left off.

CHAPTER TWO

Changing the Subject of Realism

Dreiser, Grant, Wharton

In the previous chapter, we witnessed the death of a heroine whose newly emerged desire leads her to reject the dictates of "true womanhood" and seek fulfillment through the traditionally masculine channel of liberal individualism. Fashioned to accommodate the lives of nineteenth-century middle-class men, this form of subjectivity, Chopin suggests, would not fit the nation's recently awakened middle-class women. The "awakening" that Chopin has in mind—as both the novel and her short story about Mrs. Sommers demonstrate—is inextricably linked to the transformation of womanhood that occurred as the nation shifted to a consumer economy. Once expected to be content with the comforts of a settled domesticity, middle-class women were now encouraged by the market to want much more; in fact, it depended on their doing so. They now lived in a culture that urged them to seek self-gratification while suggesting that such gratification was not to be found within the home.

But, if mother-womanhood had grown obsolete and liberal individualism was not an option, what terms remained for imagining middle-class female subjectivity? This chapter suggests that American writers after Chopin, including Theodore Dreiser, Robert

Grant, and Edith Wharton, generate entirely new ones. Dreiser's novel *Sister Carrie* (1900), Grant's *Unleavened Bread* (1900), and Wharton's *The Custom of the Country* (1913) narrate the histories of three of American literature's most socially successful heroines. From Dreiser's fictitious rural town of Columbia City, Wisconsin—a thoroughly American name signaling the protagonist's cultural representativeness—Carrie Meeber rises to preeminence on the Broadway stage. Similarly, Wharton's Undine Spragg ascends from the obscurity of her hometown of Apex—Wharton's own fabricated Midwestern nowhere suggestive of her protagonist's endless climbing—to become the wife of "one of the six wealthiest men east of the Rockies" (358). Though Grant's Selma White is less successful in New York than those two, she becomes one of the first wives on the Midwestern political scene and, by the end, appears poised to take her place among Washington's elite.

What is so striking about the prosperity of these heroines is that it neither is impelled by nor leads to the desire for freedom or self-sufficiency motivating Edna Pontellier's quest. Whereas Edna views financial independence as the means for procuring a room of her own, these later heroines accumulate wealth and status to comply with the implicit commands of their social worlds. Edna's desire is self-derived and self-directed: "I don't want anything but my own way" (650). Its tautological nature draws a tight circle around Edna, locating within the compass of her body and mind both the source and the object of her desire: She wants what she wants. In contrast, the desires of Carrie, Selma, and Undine point outward: As Undine puts it, "I want what others want" (61). Determined from without, theirs is not a desire that erects boundaries between them and the rest of the world—not one that individuates—as Edna's is. Moreover, because what they want is simply what others want, the object of their desire is fundamentally unstable, since both *what others want* and *who others are* vary.

This chapter demonstrates how Dreiser, Grant, and Wharton position this nonindividuating model of subjectivity as the replacement of liberal individualism and—what is the same thing—middle-class woman as the replacement of middle-class man in the imagining of modernity.

DREISER'S *SISTER CARRIE* AND GRANT'S *UNLEAVENED*
BREAD: THE EMERGENCE OF THE SOCIAL SELF

Though the novel bears her name, *Sister Carrie* seems as much about
her sometime lover George Hurstwood as it is about Carrie. In the
novel, her passionless romance with him is the only enduring intimate relationship in her otherwise varying life. One is moved to
wonder what business this old man has taking up so much space in
a novel putatively about the life of a budding New Woman. The fact
that Hurstwood seems to overstay his welcome in Carrie's story is
no accident, yet that does not mean that we are wrong to view him
as out of place. The seemingly disproportionate attention Dreiser
lavishes on Hurstwood is a crucial part of his attempt to redefine
the novelistic subject for a new phase of modernity.

Dreiser's novel shares this aim with another novel from 1900,
albeit one exceedingly less remembered. In *Unleavened Bread*—a
novel that Wharton put forth as a candidate for the distinction of
"Great American Novel"[1]—Grant pursues that aim through tactics
strikingly similar to Dreiser's. Since Grant's novel is now far more
obscure than Dreiser's, it requires a lengthier précis. The novel follows its implacable heroine's eventful social career, which leads her
to three different cities and into an equal number of marriages.
Selma White is obsessed with what she repeatedly refers to as her
"development," an ill-defined ambition whose vagueness renders it
no less consuming. "Her mission in life," we're told, "had promptly
been recognized by her as the development of her soul along individual lines, but until the necessity for a choice had arisen she had
been content to contemplate a little longer" (4). This presentation
of Selma's conception of development not only obscures it in im-
precise language but also defers it—a deferral that we soon learn
to understand as indefinite. In similar fashion, before accepting an
offer of marriage from her first husband—Lewis Babcock, a boorish
entrepreneur—she exacts from him a promise that he will let her
"do things," although she admits, "I don't know exactly what. It isn't
anything especial yet" (7).

Selma's insistence on aimless forward movement, on development without knowing what toward, links her with a form of desire
commonly attributed to Americans, though more frequently to men

than to women. John Kouwenhoven connects this putatively American tendency to a "concern for process rather than product"—an enduring predilection to which he accredits a wide assortment of American inventions (*Leaves of Grass*, jazz, skyscrapers, chewing gum) (133). Like Kouwenhoven, many of Grant's contemporaries celebrated this peculiarly American fetishization of the drive. In his 1881 treatise on "American nervousness," for instance, neurologist George Miller Beard finds in it the potential "for original, creative, pioneering, and productive work that shall make Europe follow us, instead of our following Europe" (xvii). As Grant's biblical title for the novel suggests, however, he was of another opinion. Unleavened bread comes to symbolize haste and slipshod work, the result of this American habit of looking forward without looking backward.[2] In portraying the nation's preoccupation with progress in so unfavorable a light, Grant aligns himself with his novel's Brahmin New Yorkers, for whom "progress presupposes in the individual or the community attaining it a prelude of slow struggle, disheartening doubts, and modest reverence for previous results—for the accumulated wisdom of the past" (372). This outlook is diametrically opposed to that held by the Selmas of the world, whose "own idea of doing things was to do them quickly and brilliantly, arriving at conclusions, as became an American, with prompt energy and despatch" (177).

As many readers have observed of Carrie, she is insatiable. The novel concludes with her fantasizing in a rocking chair—a symbol of restlessness—where, we're told, she will continue to "dream such happiness as [she] may never feel" (355). Over the years, critics have proposed a number of persuasive explanations for Carrie's inextinguishable desire—and, given the similarities between Dreiser's and Grant's novels (published in the same year), it's reasonable to assume that they might have said similar things about Selma had they written about her. Most critics, such as Rachel Bowlby and June Howard, view her insatiability as in line with the directives of consumer culture, which thrives on the proliferation of wants. Walter Benn Michaels sees it as the expression of the gold standard, a system of internal difference ("What you are is what you want, in other words, what you aren't" [42]). Jennifer Fleissner, as discussed in this book's introduction, provides an explanation based less on economics, linking the novel's open-endedness to the period's uncertainty about the future of women's lives in light of their expanding options.

In the face of such a staggering variety of interpretations, it is tempting to conclude that they must somehow negate one another. I'd like to suggest, however, that these solutions are all complementary and simply need to be constellated around a different term. The historical phenomena to which critics have attributed female insatiability in this period—the rise of consumer culture, the advent of a new economic order, the erosion of bourgeois domesticity—are each aspects of a larger historical development: the decline of individualism in the United States. In order to adapt the realist novel for an era in which the rise of associational paradigms (e.g., mass culture, corporate capitalism, vocational and avocational organizations) was rendering liberal individualism obsolete, second-generation American realists install social selves at the heart of their fictions—permeable selves capable of reflecting the kaleidoscopic society taking shape around them. This fictional subject, as we shall see, is nearly identical to the intersubjective entity emerging in the works of contemporary pragmatist philosophers, an overlap that suggests the extent to which problems of postindividualist selfhood preoccupied the American mind at the beginning of the twentieth century.[3]

Even without grasping that these writers were targeting individualism specifically, any reader familiar with nineteenth-century fiction is bound to detect something irregular in Grant's description of his heroine. In generations before Grant, the "prompt energy and despatch" ascribed to Selma were far likelier to be attributed to men. Grant was surely aware of the dissonance he created in using descriptions associated with enterprising male industrialists to characterize a comely Midwestern-born woman of the late-nineteenth century. The husbands in the novel certainly do not anticipate encountering these traits in Selma. Each views her through a rosy screen of Victorian lore, mistakenly apotheosizing her as a bona fide "angel in the house." For Babcock, Selma "symbolized . . . refinement, poetry, art, the things of the spirit" (5) and reigned as "the divinity of his domestic hearth" (12). Although her next husband, the old-guard architect Wilbur Littleton, could hardly be more different from Babcock, their expectations for Selma and conjugal life converge. To Littleton, "she appeared primarily as an object of reverence, a white-souled angel of light clad in the graceful outlines of flesh" (44). And even her shrewd third husband, a politician and lawyer, echoes his sentimental predecessors, given as he is to speaking "feelingly of the value to a public man of a stimulating and dignifying fireside" (316) and often finding himself captivated by Selma's "air suggesting poetry and high ethical resolve such as he liked to associate with her and their scheme of wedded life" (364). None of them suspects a woman who regards the loss of love as "preferable to sacrificing weakly the development of her own ideas and life to its perpetuation" (234).

The dissonance between these men's assumptions about Woman and the actual woman they encounter—a dissonance likely reproduced in some of the novel's contemporary readers—serves Grant's aim to depict a world in transition, an aim he shares with Dreiser, whose novel also incorporates such dissonance. Recall the romantic terms in which George Hurstwood—the unfortunate club manager from Chicago—thinks of Carrie. Despite overwhelming evidence to the contrary, Hurstwood "really thought, after a year, that her chief expression in life was finding its natural channel in household duties" (213).

Why do Grant and Dreiser feel compelled to narrate the story of the modern woman in so great measure as the story of modern man's confounding? In *Women, Compulsion, Modernity*, Jennifer Fleissner offers a potential solution. She asks us to distinguish between "the sentimental, which looks backward nostalgically to the past—a position [she sees] as occupied by the men in these novels—and what [she is] calling fantasy, which is oriented toward the future and associated in these texts with working women" (166). In Fleissner's dialectical conjunction, the New Woman becomes essential to the production of the "Old Man"—or, what must be the same thing, to the enervation of manhood—and she adduces Hurstwood's growing financial dependence on Carrie as evidence for this claim. However, there are a few limitations to Fleissner's explanation. For one, it risks reproducing the logic of the very view from which Fleissner rightly seeks to distance herself—the contemporary view of women's employment outside the home as robbing men of jobs.

Moreover, it cannot account for the many confounded men in novels in which there is no *economic* role reversal because the women are never wage earners, such as *Unleavened Bread*. Finally, it does not attend to the particular traits that lead to the downfalls of male characters, fates that she portrays as simply the compensatory ebbs to women's triumphant flows.[4]

These women, as Fleissner notes briefly in a later essay "Wharton, Marriage, and the New Woman," are social selves (463). The significance of this fact, as we shall see, becomes clearer once we consider the kinds of subjectivity that their social selfhood trumps. The American pragmatists of the late-nineteenth and early-twentieth century sought to formulate new paradigms of selfhood that better comported with what they viewed as a vastly altered American scene. Although William James often receives most of the credit for the invention of this revisionary conception of the self, none theorized it more systematically than sociologist George Herbert Mead. Because Mead's theory so accurately describes the selves we observe in these novels, it merits detailed elaboration here.

According to Mead, the self is dynamic and dialectical, an oscillatory entity that alternates between object of observation (*me*) and observing subject (*I*). Mead suggests that we begin as objects gazed at by the social world and eventually become subjects through learning how to view ourselves from social cues (such as facial gestures of disapproval and approval). Since, in reflecting on our own actions, we repeatedly adopt the attitudes of others whom we remember to have observed us in a similar situation, we learn to see ourselves and our actions as our observers had. Adopting our observers' attitudes toward comportment, we end up reproducing those behaviors that we remember to have been viewed with approval and eschewing those that have been met with disapproval. The result is that we seem imitative.

Given that the actions of social selves are guided by the desire for approval, we should not be surprised that such beings remain constantly in pursuit of being "well-liked"—the designation that Warren Susman's classic study of Gilded Age America posits as the gold standard in a "culture of personality." Indeed, Selma at one point tells her beleaguered second husband, "To make people like one is the way to get business, I believe" (212). Throughout their stories, both Selma and Carrie are governed by their other-directedness, so much so that it even shapes their avid consumerism, a preoccupation that is often denigrated as solipsistic, especially in women. Even those who take a less obviously disapproving view of women and consumption—such as Bowlby, for instance—still regard it as narcissistic.[5] While scholars frequently view the commodity as a vehicle for indulging fantasies of self-transformation (whether they see this as good or bad), they seldom note how socially driven consumer habits were often imagined to be. They overlook, in other words, the fact that these visions of self-transformation are often motivated by a perceived discrepancy between the person the consumer presently is and the person whom she intuits her ever-changing social milieu would like her to be. When, for example, Selma first calls on a lady of East Coast refinement, she covets that lady's attire precisely because of such a discrepancy, thinking that her "white, starched cuffs seemed to make light of her own sober, unadorned wrists" (32). Similarly, when, after weeks of isolation in New York, Carrie finally begins to interact with people other than Hurstwood, she begins to note discrepancies that stir her desire: "She also saw that she was not well dressed—not nearly as well dressed—as Mrs. Vance. . . . Her situation was cleared up for her. She felt that her life was becoming stale, and therein she felt cause for gloom. . . . The desirous Carrie was whispered to concerning her possibilities" (216). Though the rise of consumer culture undeniably helped establish the conditions for conceiving of women as desire-ridden, a focus on the fetishistic dimension of commodity culture simply cannot tell us the whole story.[6] Moreover, both novels seem to anticipate the possibility that readers might mistake the socially motivated desires of their protagonists for naked materialism. Grant does so by telling us, after revealing that Selma is to receive an unexpected twenty thousand dollars from a dying nonrelative, the money "seemed of secondary importance" to the opportunity for social display that overseeing his bequest of a free hospital would afford. Dreiser distances Carrie from mere acquisitiveness more directly, with his laconic summary of her conception of money: "Money: something everybody else has and I must get" (45). For her, money derives its value solely from the fact of everyone else's having it; currency matters to her because it keeps her current.

We have seen that Grant's and Dreiser's protagonists are social selves, but what does that mean for the realist novel? The work of historian James Livingston equips us to address this question. In *Pragmatism, Feminism, and Democracy*, Livingston connects the pragmatists' reenvisioning of modern subjectivity to the "'socialization' of modern industry via corporate devices" and "the implication of the family in a new universe of 'social organizations'" near the turn of the twentieth century (11). This transformation was driving American society away from individualistic forms of self-definition and toward more associational forms. As a result, for pragmatist thinkers, the "pressing intellectual problem was . . . to posit a form of subjectivity consistent with the 'change of social life from an individual to a corporate affair'" (81). In positioning the social self as the "solvent" of liberal individualism, Livingston reveals that what this new form of subjectivity trumps is no less than the form that had predominated in Western philosophy and culture since John Locke's foundational writings. Grant's and Dreiser's novels indicate that, in 1900, American novelists began doing for realist fiction what the pragmatists were doing for philosophy, replacing individualism with models of selfhood more compatible with twentieth-century modernity.

As elaborated in the book's introduction, literary scholars have long associated the realist novel with liberal individualism, at least since Ian Watt's seminal *The Rise of the Novel* (1957). Unlike most field-shaping premises, this conviction has only deepened over the years, despite decades of methodological shifts. To be clear, in invoking the concept of individualism, I emphatically do not have in mind some simplistic notion of a self-absorbed, antisocial maverick, such as that commonly associated with Jacksonian-era frontiersmanship or, mistakenly, with Emersonian self-reliance. Rather, I refer to the "profoundly cerebral and privatized subject" who emerges in Elaine Hadley's study of mid-Victorian culture—the very kind of subject that we see defended no less sedulously in the novels of the United States' most vociferous exponent of realism, William Dean Howells (20). This subject is, as Nancy Armstrong has shown, self-enclosed and impermeable, his feelings and desires originating solely from within rather than invading from without (*How Novels Think* 12–20). The pervasiveness of this figure in nineteenth-century realism impels Armstrong, as we have seen, to the apodictic claim that "new varieties of novel cannot help taking up the project of universalizing the individual subject. That, simply put, is what novels do" (10).

It is clear, however, that Grant and Dreiser believed that the realist novel could and must dispense with the liberal individual if it was to remain relevant in twentieth-century America. This conviction is apparent not only in the extroverted (turned-outward) social selves who serve as their protagonists but also in their handling of male individualists. In both of these novels, male characters are portrayed as the hapless, love-starved casualties of their female lovers' quests for fulfillment. What may seem little more than a battle between the sexes is, in fact, part of a complex strategy for staging a confrontation between an outmoded literary and philosophical paradigm and a newer one. As we have seen, the male characters' views about marriage and women are plucked directly from nineteenth-century gender ideology. They idealize women as domestic divinities and marriage as a completing ritual, the culmination of self-development and the end of all striving. For one of Grant's men, marriage constitutes "perfect satisfaction" (13), and another predicts that he and Selma will "be all and all to each other spiritually as husband and wife" (106).

Many readers have also noted Hurstwood's old-fashioned idealization of conjugal life, remarking on the fact that he, in Amy Kaplan's oft-quoted formulation, pursues "Carrie less for a risqué liaison than for a cozy domesticity" (*Social Construction* 144). Lest it seem that Grant and Dreiser were merely parodying the conventions of nineteenth-century domestic fiction—rather than clearing space for a new vision of the social world—we should recall how fundamental this older view of marriage and domesticity was to liberal individualism. According to Gillian Brown, "Nineteenth-century American individualism takes on its peculiarly 'individualistic' properties as domesticity inflects it with values of interiority, privacy, and psychology" (1). The romanticized ways in which these men conceive of women and domesticity mirror the logic on which the nineteenth century's "separate spheres" ideology was based, an ideology that shaped that era's conception of modern subjectivity.

In addition to portraying these men's notions of conjugality as relics of a bygone age, Grant and Dreiser also oppose the rigid structure of their desire to the radically open-ended form exhibited by their heroines. In their male characters, the novelists circumscribe desire within the confines of their minds and bodies; moreover, their desires point to clear, stable objects and are therefore satiable. This can be observed in the exalted terms in which they envision marriage, construing it as the supreme antidote to desire. Grant draws a tight circle around Selma's second husband in describing his "ambitions" as "definite and congenial," fixed and deriving entirely from within him (156). In a single stroke, Grant establishes Littleton's satiability and impermeability, hallmarks of the self-possessed individual of liberal philosophy. Dreiser is even more emphatic about the definiteness of Hurstwood's desire, devoting much of the story to tracing its gradual contraction to basic need: "There was something sad in realising that, after all, all that he wanted of her was something to eat" (274). It just doesn't get more definite than that.

The well-defined, internally derived desires of Littleton and Hurstwood are a far cry from the promiscuous, contagion-like ones that invade Selma and Carrie, propelling them toward everything but satisfaction. Selma's fixation on development keeps her developing without ever becoming developed, her sense of that term shifting each time she enters a new social setting. Even desires thought to be inmost are shown in Selma to have their origins wholly in the social world, the products of perceived discrepancies between her present self and the idealized selves frenetically circulating about her. For example, her desire for children results not from some innate inclination toward motherhood—as Littleton mistakenly imagines—but from social envy. While she gazes through the window at the well-dressed children of her fashionable neighbor (aptly nicknamed "Flossy"), the "thought of how prettily she would have been able to dress a baby of her own was at times so pathetic as to bring tears to her eyes, and cause her to deplore her own lack of children as a misfortune" (187). At this revelation, we cannot help recalling, even if Selma does not, the deceased infant from her first marriage, whom she hardly mourns and whose death seemed almost welcome for enabling her to replace an ambition that had grown stale (motherhood) with a budding new one (social activism). The social provenances of Carrie's desires are equally apparent, her mind likened to "a mirror prepared of her own and the world's opinions" (66).

In a world so rich in social possibilities, the permeability of Grant's and Dreiser's heroines guarantees the insatiability of their desire. Indeed, the paucity of society to which the delay of literary realism in the United States has long been attributed had, by the turn of the century, given way to great complexity—socioeconomically, ethnically, and professionally. For social selves such as Selma and Carrie, as the persistence of Selma's watchword "development" suggests, this complexity created the conditions for limitless mutability and inextinguishable desire. The opportunities to perceive discrepancies between themselves and their social environs abounded in the variegated cultural landscapes they inhabited. What is more, this insatiability makes it impossible to assimilate these heroines into the individualist framework of the nineteenth-century realist novel, for it renders them incapable of moving their status from the present progressive to the past perfect: They are always developing and never developed.

As suggested by the idealizations of conjugality in Grant's and Dreiser's male characters, the individual in the nineteenth-century novel becomes an individual in the first place through his disciplined capacity to restrict his desires to the demands of adulthood. Once all its major demands have been met—the establishment of a vocation and a nuclear family—he is supposed to be satisfied. The transcendental bliss of the bourgeois home is his reward for exchanging his youthful unrest for the sober satisfactions of adulthood.[7] However, the enduring satisfaction that awaits the good subject of nineteenth-century realism becomes unthinkable in heroines whose wishes are tethered to a kaleidoscopic social world. Moreover, their insatiability preempts narrative closure, in a way that anticipates a major development in the modernist novel.[8] Hence, both novels conclude not with "the sense of an ending" but in scenes of longing. The final sentence of *Unleavened Bread* has Selma "gazing straight before her with her far away, seraph look, as though she were penetrating the future even into Paradise" (431). Not even her elevation to senator's wife can keep her eyes from seeking after the next big thing. Similarly, Dreiser's well-known sentous ending prophesies that Carrie will continue rocking in her chair, dreaming of such happiness as she "may never feel" (355).

Walter Benn Michaels accurately views satisfaction as "the sign of incipient failure, decay, and finally death" in *Sister Carrie,* and it operates in much the same way in *Unleavened Bread* (42). It is in this respect that the novels most savagely signal the end of individualism. While narrating the staggering successes of their desiring heroines, both novels expel their satiable male characters, linking their demises to what Grant describes as the definiteness of their desire and the fixity of their egos. Littleton stakes so much on married life that the failure of his marriage with Selma positively crushes him. Grant underscores this fact by having Littleton die of heart failure—a somewhat unsubtle way of establishing the severity of his heartbreak. Dreiser, as we have seen, traces the diminution of Hurstwood's desire, and he follows this descending trajectory to its extreme: the eradication in Hurstwood of the very desire for self-preservation. Ultimately, Hurstwood might be said to have taken his own life, but Dreiser's handling of the scene demands a slightly more nuanced interpretation. During his final night, Hurstwood turns on the gas in his flea-bitten room without applying fire to it. As the fumes reach his nostrils, there is no literary embrace of quietus—none of Juliet's "O happy dagger"—but, rather, a passive disinclination to intervene in his own behalf. His final words are "What's the use?" and these he mutters "weakly, as he stretched himself to rest" (353). As Dreiser's scripting suggests, it is less that Hurstwood desires death than that he *does not desire* life.

Grant's and Dreiser's novels are at one in their conviction that nineteenth-century individualism had to give place to a more permeable and more mutable form of subjectivity. For all their similarities, however, their respective attempts to reconceive the modern subject diverge in one significant way. Whereas Grant emphasizes Selma's inexorable drive and attributes her success to that indomitable force, Dreiser makes much of Carrie's passivity. Although Selma's desires invade her from the social world and are constantly shifting, she nonetheless pursues them, as we have seen, with the "prompt energy and despatch" that she believes "became an American." Carrie, on the other hand, is described as being "of a passive and receptive rather than an active and aggressive nature" (212). Indeed, serendipities just seem to happen to her, largely because of her passivity. It is an extemporaneous, purely accidental pout that initiates her wildly successful acting career on Broadway. Though this divide may appear a stumbling block in American novelists' attempt to renovate realism, the conflict between Selma's drive and Carrie's passivity proved remarkably generative for one of Grant and Dreiser's most eminent contemporaries, Edith Wharton, to whom we now turn.

THE CONSUMMATION OF THE SOCIAL SELF: EDITH WHARTON'S *THE CUSTOM OF THE COUNTRY*

In *Unleavened Bread,* Grant frequently refers to Selma's excessive patriotism and obsession with Americanness. These references hint at Grant's intention to portray her not as idiosyncratic but as representative of the spirit of the nation. Similarly, in the next decade, Wharton used her insatiable heroine, whose initials are U. S., to represent "the custom of the country." Critics have tended to interpret *The Custom of the Country* as a satire on early-twentieth-century society. They suggest that Undine represents all that Wharton hated about the period. The critical tendency to vilify Undine is often subtly misogynistic—a surprising fact, given that many of the exponents of this view are self-identified feminist critics. For instance, Candace Waid understands the novel as Wharton's allegory of the impossibility of creating art in America. In this interpretation, Wharton's artistic aristocrat Ralph Marvell, in falling for Undine, falls victim to a "false muse" (131). In his pursuit of transcendent art, according to Waid, he permits himself to be taken in by hollow artifice, the supposed predicament facing any aesthete forced to rely on American culture for artistic nourishment. In similar fashion, Janet Malcolm describes Undine as "Becky Sharp stripped of all charm, spirit, and warmth, the adventuress pared down to her pathology" (11).

However, if Undine is as bad we are told—and she can be pretty bad—shouldn't the fact that Marvell pursues such a manifestly unworthy object cast him in just as unfavorable a light? Moreover,

Wharton herself was an aesthete who relied on American culture for artistic nourishment, yet she managed well enough. Pessimistic interpretations of the novel that fixate on Undine's shortcomings (and, again, they are many) miss how inspiring Wharton found her historical moment, glossing over Wharton's disdain-tinged fascination with the new character type embodied by her heroine. They unconsciously recast the author in the role of reactionary "great dame," a stereotype that Wharton scholars have diligently worked to overthrow.[9] If we are to pursue the novel's most interesting questions, we must move beyond the fixation on what Undine lacks so that we can consider what she contains.

Situating Wharton among her contemporaries helps get us there. Marvell is the spitting image of Robert Grant's Wilbur Littleton—artistic, sensitive, a lasting relic of a declining New York aristocracy. Like Littleton, Marvell belongs to a sizeable group of old-fashioned male characters who cling to bygone ideals about women and domesticity, so much so that the dissolution of Ralph's marriage practically dissolves him (he kills himself). Littleton thinks Selma "an original soul, ignorant and unenlightened perhaps, but endowed with swift perception and capable of noble development" (44). In similar fashion, Ralph Marvell takes Undine's frankness and pliability for signs of a rare responsiveness that would flourish in conjugal life.

Like his predecessors in Dreiser's and Grant's novels, however, Marvell greatly mistakes his mistress. In *The Custom of the Country*, Wharton offers us yet another dramatization of the shifting notions of selfhood we see in the early-twentieth century, which pit insatiable female social selves against rigid male liberal individuals. But her affiliation with the old guard of New York society makes her more sensitive to some of the implications this shift had for class hierarchy in the United States—implications lost on her more middle-class contemporaries. Undine and her parents are the picture of the parvenu family, belonging to that class of people to whom one of Wharton's characters refers as "the Invaders" (48). Thanks to Mr. Spraggs's shrewd business speculations in Apex, they are able to move from their remote Midwestern town to the heart of New York City, into a gilded suite at the Stentorian, where they hope to give Undine a wider field of suitors. As social climbers, these conspicuous consumers staunchly believe in the power of appearances, a conviction that playing the part is tantamount to being it.

Wharton's friend and literary forerunner Henry James—also descended of the old guard—briefly explores the social reorganization propelled by this new-moneyed group. In James's allegorical short story "The Real Thing" (1892), an artist relates his encounter with the Monarchs, a pair of impoverished aristocrats who hope to earn money by modeling for some of his illustrations. Out of pity, he hires them for a few sittings. But he finds them too "stiff" for his purposes, too uncompromisingly themselves to serve as models for figures of whom they were not. For instance, the narrator tells us that Mrs. Monarch "was always a lady certainly, and into the bargain was always the same lady. She was the real thing, but always the same thing" (200). His preferred models—even for illustrations of regal characters, ironically—are a pair of working-class models, a "freckled cockney" and an Italian emigrant. The lady is suggestively named Miss Churm, a bastardized form of one of the keywords of the culture of personality, *charm*. The artist values Miss Churm for "the fact that she had no positive stamp, combined of course with the other fact that what she did have was a curious and inexplicable talent for imitation" (200).

Her vaunted plasticity is characteristic of this historical moment, when people were prospering in unprecedented numbers by appearing as others wanted them to. The narrator's curious declaration elevating appearance above essence—"I liked things that appeared; then one was sure"—seems axiomatic for the period (195). (This echoes Carrie's paradoxical reaction to the stage—"Here was no illusion" [123].) James drives this point home by having life imitate art: Impostors replace the real things not just in paintings but in the social hierarchy as well. By the end of the story, the aristocratic Monarchs are waiting on the models, bringing them tea and fixing their hair. In this radical reversal, the posers have supplanted their referents. The real thing has become the servant of the counterfeit.

We witness a similar reversal in *The Custom of the Country*, but Wharton portrays it less ruefully than James does. The Monarchs beg to stay on with the artist and work as domestics, but he simply cannot face this travesty: "I couldn't—it was dreadful to see them emptying my slops" (210). In his aversion, the artist speaks for an

outraged James. The author, too, averts his gaze from the impostors, relegating Miss Churm to the story's margins and expressing
his disdain for the culture she represents through the slurring of
one of its central values: *charm* is garbled into *churm*, which sounds
like *churn*. James was more interested—as he would be again in
The American Scene—in what was being unmade at this historical
juncture than in what was being made.[10] Wharton took this same
view in her first novel, *The House of Mirth* (1905). It's nigh impossible
to forget the provocative reflection in her autobiography, which
contains the sentence that has become synonymous with her name:
"A frivolous society can acquire dramatic significance only through
what its frivolity destroys" (*Backward Glance* 940). In *The Custom of
the Country*, however, Wharton faces this transformation head-on,
abandoning her elegiac attitude to examine what it produces rather
than what it "destroys."

Accordingly, she takes Undine, the posturing upstart, as the novel's focal point rather than the besieged patricians, "the real thing."
Although Undine never becomes a professional actress, as Carrie
does, she is described chiefly through the language of performance.
According to the narrator, "She might have been some fabled creature whose home was a ray of light" (14). A woman ever on display,
Undine carries Bishop Berkeley's famous declaration that "To be
is to be perceived" to its literal extreme. For her, image is all. When
first invited to dinner by Ralph's sister, Undine asks bemusedly,
"Isn't it queer? Why does *she* want me? She's never seen me!" and,
according to the narrator, "Her tone implied that she had long been
accustomed to being 'wanted' by those who had" (6). With unflagging faith in the power and primacy of image, Undine is completely
at a loss to understand how she can be of any interest to—or even
have an existence in the mind of—anyone who has not had the privilege of looking at her.

Wharton's fixation on appearance in characterizing Undine directly contrasts with her mode of describing the members of the
old guard. As Nancy Bentley points out, Ralph belongs to "the race
of *subjects*, of fulsome interior selves" (*Ethnography* 176). The narrator likens his subjectivity to the intricate, mysterious cave that
he discovers as a boy and subsequently guards as his own private
possession. This "secret inaccessible place with glaucous lights,

mysterious murmurs, and a single shaft of communication with the sky" symbolizes the rich interior world that he aspires to share with the right woman, "'made,'" as he is, "for conjugal bliss" (47–48).

Made for conjugal bliss: Wharton's scare quotes help draw attention to another important distinction between the older individualistic form of subjectivity and the extroverted form used to characterize the new modern subject. Just as the cave metaphor conveys inwardness and depth—which contrast with Undine's superficiality, her outwardness—the conceit also signals the ontological rigidity of Ralph's kind. It reminds us of James's inflexible aristocratic models. While Ralph is "made" for conjugal bliss, Mrs. Monarch is described as a lady "who's already made" (197). Like Dreiser's Hurstwood and the men of *Unleavened Bread*, Ralph's self-formation is teleological and oriented toward closure and satisfaction. For him, as for the rich characters of classical realism, there is a final point of individual development, which entails a thorough self-possession. This is why he views entering into the workforce as alienating: It is tantamount to having "sold his brains to the firm" (173); likewise, he describes "uncongenial work" as "killing" to a man (197). In addition to his individualist ideas about work and self-possession, he maintains the Victorian faith in the transformative powers of wedlock, believing that marriage will fulfill both him and Undine and banish all desire from their lives permanently: "One day, of course, someone would discover [his cave] and reign there with him—no, reign over it and him" (47). In Ralph's view, marriage represents the self's culmination, beyond which there is nothing.

However, for the character wont to lament that "it was always her fate to find out just too late about the 'something beyond,'" no such culminations exist, most certainly not in an ambitious marriage meant to win her wealth and admiration (34). Desire in Undine remains endlessly proliferative, such that, as Jean-Michel Rabaté points out, "she produces desire all the time and hence the means to acquire its objects, without being interested in the enjoyment that possession is supposed to bring" (192). But to conclude therefore, as Rabaté does, that "what she is after is . . . the drive" would be to exaggerate the agency of this obsessively imitative character. As Bentley observes (anticipating Fleissner's notion of "compulsion"), Undine's drive results not from independent will but from a curious blend of will and social forces: "Undine's agency of 'nerve' represents a cathexis of social forces and personal disposition: the two are never collapsed, but neither can they be 'sorted'" (*Ethnography* 174).[11] In other words, the novel, like pragmatist philosophy, complicates agency to the point where it makes little sense to talk about what Undine is "after," since the distinction between what she chooses to pursue and what she is involuntarily drawn to has been eliminated once and for all. As calculating and industrious as Undine appears once she has a goal in mind, the novel goes to great lengths to show that the all-consuming desire propelling her in any given situation originates entirely from without: recall her confession, "I want what others want" (61).

The narrator tells us that "Undine was fiercely independent and yet passionately imitative. She wanted to surprise every one by her dash and originality, but she could not help modelling herself on the last person she met . . ." (13). Mead's theory of the social self helps us decode Undine's paradoxical form of agency, an admixture of social determination and willfulness. In premising subjectivity on objectification (individuals must exist as objects gazed at in order to learn how to gaze at themselves) and proposing an ongoing oscillation between the two poles, the theory of the social self deeply entwines individual desire and drive with the social world. It produces the kind of endlessly shifting, socially determined desire that Undine sums up in her declaration "I want what others want." She is a social being who develops self-consciousness through viewing her reflection in the eyes of others: "The image of herself in other minds . . . was her only notion of self-seeing" (245); "What Undine really enjoyed was the image of her own charm mirrored in the general admiration" (96). And the paradoxes inhering in the form of selfhood we see in Undine virtually explode our prevailing taxonomies of literary character. In her otherwise perceptive study of the parvenu in turn-of-the-century American literature, Stephanie Foote misses this point, construing the parvenu figure as "a flat character, without depth or motive, without the interiority" (6). This may be true for the many unsuccessful parvenus that Foote discusses, but it is certainly not so for Undine. Constantly shapeshifting in response to her constantly shapeshifting desires, she is neither flat nor round, neither static nor dynamic—or else she is both at once. Either way one chooses to view the matter, Undine's character unsettles our literary classifications just as much as she unsettles the class boundaries of her day.

What initially seem bold, self-directed enterprises on Undine's part turn out to be socially compelled quests for approval and celebrity—the stuff of personality rather than personhood. In the kind of social selfhood represented by Undine, we find a literalization of one of the core tenets of the culture of personality. In the early-twentieth-century society of "performing" selves that Susman sketches, the measure of personality is whether one is "well-liked," whether one is a "Somebody" (280, 277). To be, therefore, is not merely to be perceived but to be *well* perceived. Far from the autonomous selfhood and isolated interiority represented by old-fashioned characters like Ralph and his family, Undine's social selfhood stands glaringly in opposition to the teleological arcs of subjective development characterizing classical realism. Brought up in a world that understood selfhood as something eventually arrived at rather than something always in flux, Ralph cannot see Undine for what she really is. Like Dreiser's sententious narrator who can envision for Carrie no trajectory beyond the two linear paths of progress and decline,[12] Ralph believes that either he will be able to save Undine—like a Perseus to an imperiled Andromeda, to adapt his metaphor—or "the girl's very sensitiveness to new impressions, combined with her obvious lack of any sense of relative values, would make her an easy prey to the powers of folly" (51). Ralph's charitable interpretation of Undine's malleability echoes Wilbur Littleton's early impression of Selma in *Unleavened Bread*: "Here, he said to himself, was an original soul, ignorant and unenlightened perhaps, but endowed with swift perception and capable of noble development" (44). Nothing in their experience has prepared these two old-fashioned aristocrats for the mutable women who now prevail, and so both men are thrown back on hackneyed ideas about feminine impressionableness in their attempts to decipher their beloveds.

As I have been suggesting, men's failure to understand women is a recurring theme in this period's fiction. We saw an early instance of this trend in Kate Chopin's "A Pair of Silk Stockings," when the newly self-indulgent protagonist confounds her male fellow passenger on the cable car. Dreiser's Hurstwood interprets Carrie through the outmoded lens of Victorian domestic ideology and, in the process, greatly misconstrues her. Wilbur Littleton and Ralph Marvell mistake their wives' uncanny social instincts for evidence of a poetic receptiveness that would flourish under the proper guidance (namely, theirs). Depicting the relations between the sexes in this way—as an unending series of misrecognitions on men's part—enables these authors to signal a changing of the guards in the cultural vision of modernity. The new modern subject, these novels suggest, is like nothing American culture had ever seen, and understanding this subject would require a set of terms alien to the mind of the nineteenth-century liberal individual.

As if confounding each of their individualistic male characters weren't enough, these novelists make their rejection of the liberal subject crystal clear by killing them all off. All three men die in acts of resignation, practically acknowledging their unfitness for modern America. Hurstwood dejectedly asks, "What's the use?" before fatally turning up the gas in his fifteen-cent hotel room. Before Ralph fires the revolver through his skull, he capitulates to Undine's wish for the dissolution of the marriage: "My wife," he says to himself, "this will make things right for her" (290). And, though Littleton does not commit suicide, he dies of heart failure—a failure of heart—which the novel invites us to understand as his surrender to a world so at odds with his old-fashioned ideals.

CELEBRITY AND THE BREAKDOWN OF PROGRESS IN
THE CUSTOM OF THE COUNTRY

By way of conclusion, I'd like to examine an aspect of the period's contemplation of the new modern subject that Wharton's novel develops further than Dreiser's and Grant's, probably because it was written a few years later into the twentieth century. The expansion of visual technologies in this period enables Wharton to probe yet another premise of classical liberal ideology. Earlier conceptions of progress entwined material advancement with growth in less visible spheres of human life—intellectual, spiritual, moral. As her early description of Undine hints—"she might have been some fabled creature whose home was a ray of light"—Wharton was preoccupied with the intensification of visual culture in her day, a moment that witnessed the birth of cinema and the concomitant emergence of the celebrity. The accelerated expansion of the visual landscape in the early-twentieth century spurred Wharton and some of her contemporaries to rethink the perennial equation of material with individual progress—a phenomenon deeply related to the alterations to the public sphere at the center of Bentley's study of mass culture.[13] As they observed the visible world grow at an astonishing rate, they began to doubt that the inner life could keep pace.

To unravel the idea of progress, Wharton portrays the modern subject as schismatic, a being whose inner and outer lives are things virtually apart. Wharton was neither the first nor the last to suggest such a schism. It was central to the thinking of some of her contemporaries, including Henry James and Georg Simmel, and would figure significantly in much later accounts of postmodernism.[14] (We have seen this notion at play in *Sister Carrie* as well: Carrie's ultimate financial success, as noted above, does not correspond to moral or spiritual growth.) Once again, a comparison between Wharton and James helps illustrate the divergence of Wharton's generation of realists from their predecessors. In his 1907 travelogue of the United States, *The American Scene*, James inveighs against the breakdown of the liberal idea of progress with a good deal of asperity. According to James, unlike Old World cities, where subjective life had grown in accord with the object world (Zola's Paris is his example), American urban space, in its "boundless immensity," had "got ahead of . . . any possibility of poetic, of dramatic capture" (425). Boastful of its inordinate productivity, the scene speaks to James, intoning, "See what I'm making of all this—see what I'm making, what I'm making." Swelled with "the eloquence of [his] exasperation," he rejoins forcefully, "I see what you are *not* making, oh, what you are ever so vividly not . . ." (734).

Wharton, on the other hand, was much less concerned with what this culture was *not* making. *The Custom of the Country*—which at least one preeminent literary critic has hailed as Wharton's "best book" (Bloom 637)—is one among many novels of the time demonstrating that, for some, postindividualist American society was, contra James, far from exceeding "any possibility of poetic . . . capture." Indeed, Wharton recognizes what this cultural shift was obliterating, but she retains the remnants of the old culture less to elegize them than to emphasize what replaces them. Ralph Marvell's patrician family is a signal example. We are told that they are "so closely identified with the old house in Washington Square that they might have passed for its inner consciousness as it might have stood for their outward form" (45). This intimate rapport between subjects and their objects—what Bill Brown, in a different context, calls "the indeterminate ontology where things seem slightly human and humans seem slightly thing-like" (13)—is opposed to "the social disintegration expressed by widely-different architectural physiognomies at the other end of Fifth Avenue," home to the showy nouveau riche (45).

The severance of interior life from external reality for which Fifth Avenue society acts as proxy is part of the novel's rejection of classical liberalism, which flourished in a culture wedded to the belief that material and subjective progress went hand in hand. In its profound swerve away from realism's stabilizing harmonization of interior with exterior, *The Custom of the Country*, like James and others, points to an incoherency of culture. At one moment, Ralph compares his "singularly coherent and respectable" set to the "chaos and indiscriminate appetites which made up modern tendencies" (45). As many scholars of the English novel have demonstrated (Armstrong and Michael McKeon, most notably), the realist novel was complicit with a rising bourgeois ideology that transformed "the body from an indicator of rank to the container of a unique subjectivity" (Armstrong, *How Novels Think* 4). In doing so, it propounded individual merit and virtue instead of heredity as the requirements for social prominence and prosperity (hence its conflation of subjective growth with material advancement). In the production-oriented world of classical liberalism, the individual's accomplishments were the outer expression of his latent virtues.

In Undine, we see exactly the opposite: Subjective vacuity is the condition of her social advancement (shades of Warhol). Like James's Miss Churm, her value lies in "the fact that she had no positive stamp" ("Real Thing" 200). Characterized by "freshness" and "malleability," like Carrie, Undine has passivity and adaptability where more old-fashioned characters like Ralph have rich interiority and an anchored sense of self (50). Undine and Ralph's

honeymoon in Italy is meant to leave us in no doubt of her empti-
ness, lest we mistake her social success for evidence of traditional
forms of merit. In contrast to Ralph's active, philosophical mind
(he spends most of the trip contemplating his book), "Her mind
was as destitute of beauty and mystery as the prairie school house
on which she had been educated" (90). Thus, while Ralph revels in
the Sienese landscape and the splendor of his new bride, Undine
complains of the heat, piqued only by the prospect of mingling
with whatever society the city afforded. Here he begins to suspect,
however vaguely, that her "*diverse et ondoyante*" qualities may not,
after all, evince the poetic potential with which his imagination
had endued them: "He had seen her face droop as he suggested
the possibility of an escape from the crowds in Switzerland, and it
came to him, with the sharpness of a knife-thrust, that a crowd was
what she wanted—that she was sick to death of being alone with
him" (89–90). For Ralph, marriage is the source of satisfaction and
an overall sense of completion—the final touch in the construction
of a robust subjectivity. For Undine, however, it is merely one point
on an unending journey of compulsive self-fashioning—and, as her
staggering pattern of divorces demonstrates, there is nothing final
about it.

In keeping with its separation of inner reality from outer, as it repeatedly highlights Undine's subjective vacuity, the novel also magnifies her physical image to monstrous proportions—proportions
entirely incommensurate with her hollow interiority. Interestingly,
the importance Undine places on image cultivation and the astonishing number of media through which she manages to disseminate
her image make her an interesting prototype for the celebrity of an
even more visual age, postmodern culture. Examining the rise of celebrity in an age of proliferating visual technologies, Wendy Steiner
defines celebrities as "real people who earn a living by generating
images of themselves" (*Real Real Thing* 47). And, though Undine is
certainly no wage earner, her social career and career as a social self
are advanced through successfully propagating her image—a feat
that involves the even greater one of collapsing *being* with *seeming*.

One of the first major indications of this aspect of Undine's identity is her great affinity for the ridiculously named society portrait
artist Claud Walsingham Popple, at the mention of whom "the pink

in her cheeks deepened" (22). Even though he is an artist hired by
the wealthy to reproduce their likenesses for posterity, instead of
portraying their models, his portraits, as Ralph's mother observes,
"seem to proclaim what a gentleman he is, and how he fascinates
women. They're not pictures of Mrs. or Miss So-and-so, but simply
of the impression that Popple thinks he's made on them" (22). Later,
upon the completion of Undine's own society portrait, Peter Van
Degen—one of the leading figures of the upstart class dubbed "the
Invaders"—takes the occasion to sum up what he and his kind look
for in art and, as it turns out, in life as well:

> Hang it . . . the great thing in a man's portrait is to catch the like-
> ness—we all know that; but with a woman's it's different—a wom-
> an's picture has got to be pleasing. Who wants it about if it isn't?
> Those big chaps who blow about what they call realism—how do
> *their* portraits look in a drawing-room? Do you suppose they ever
> ask themselves that? *They* don't care—they're not going to live with
> the things! And what do they know of drawing-rooms, anyhow? Lots
> of them haven't even got a dress-suit. There's where old Popp has
> the pull over 'em—*he* knows how we live and what we want. (119)

According to Van Degen, it is the artist prone to compromising au-
thenticity for a "pleasing" image who knows how his kind lives and
what they want. As the women crowd around the portrait, with a
feeling equal parts admiration and envy, one of the more faultfind-
ing viewers complains that "it looks like a last year's dress" (120). But
Van Degen, with a rather peculiar reply, explains that her quibble
is beside the point: "It doesn't look like a last year's face, anyhow"
(120). Apparently, every part of the image, even something as defining as the face, is as malleable and modish as fashion, and Popple's
ability to manipulate even the most essential of its aspects is, in this
milieu, the mark of his craftsmanship.

Delighted by all the praise her image earns at the party, Undine
seeks to expand her circle of admiration even farther, deciding "to
stop on the way home and telephone her press-agent to do a para-
graph about Popple's tea" (121). As if the life-size portrait weren't
enlargement enough, Undine magnifies and multiplies her image more still by essentially disseminating an image of an image

(a circulated write-up about a portrait), extending her image two virtual removes from her actual person. Despite their virtuality, her proliferated images prove astoundingly potent. While she is an ocean away with her soon-to-be new husband in France, Ralph remains maddeningly haunted by "photographs of Undine," "effigies of all shapes and sizes, expressing every possible sentiment dear to the photographic tradition" (207). Significantly, they all "throned over his other possessions as her *image* had throned over his future the night he had sat in that very room and dreamed of soaring up with her into the blue . . ." (208; italics mine but ellipsis Wharton's). Just before he takes his own life, even though Undine is nowhere near him, Ralph is besieged by "that overwhelming sense of her physical nearness," and his final thought before pulling the trigger is that "this will make it all right for her" (288, 290). The aforementioned "cave" that Wharton uses earlier as a metaphor for his deep subjectivity has degenerated into the nightmare of Plato's allegory of the cave—an infinite regress from the real.

As her images move farther and farther away from her own physical presence, developing a hyperreal life of their own in circulation, the Undine phenomenon begins to resemble an early version of what Jean Baudrillard would diagnose decades later as the "precession of the simulacra." Baudrillard argues that postmodern culture witnessed a radical reversal in the traditional semiotic situation: Signs and images have wrested priority from the real things that they purport to represent. An all-powerful sign that only nominally represents the real, the simulacrum wins for itself a nonreferential life in which "the difference between 'true' and 'false'" hardly figures (1,734). And what this means is that, in the world of the simulacrum, image is all: Whether or not it accurately represents its putative referent, it demands to be taken seriously and has a *real*, autonomous presence in the world—one so potent that it not just competes with but completely erases its would-be referent.

Although Wharton's novel does not share Baudrillard's heavy note of elegy, the similarities between his simulacrum and her pyrotechnic heroine are unmistakable: Exterior image and putative referent are barely related. Undine's brilliancy has nothing to do with the person behind the paintings and social columns and everything to do with the media themselves—with the persuasiveness

of her image. The dazzling vivacity and fullness of the images pur-
porting to advertise Undine mask an imitative creature of desire
far less ample than her press would suggest. Even those closest to
her are forced to settle for a diluted intimacy with her scintillating
surface since, of course, there's little else. We have already seen
how Undine's image "throned" over Ralph's life, but he is certainly
not alone. At the end of the novel, when Undine's only child, Paul,
asks about the mother from whom boarding school has left him
estranged, Mrs. Heeney, the family's manicurist, reads him a series of clippings from social columns detailing the prices Undine
and Elmer Moffatt paid for various things. When Paul protests,
"I'd rather hear about my mother" (357), she reads him a clipping
reporting the cost paid for her new pearl necklace, believing that
this would come closer to the mark since it was specifically about
one of *her* items. Naturally, although "he didn't quite know how to
frame his question" (357), Paul did not want to hear about "their
things," so he importunes Mrs. Heeney further, in hopes of obtain-
ing even the slightest glimpse into his mother's subjective world.
By the end of the scene, however, young Paul is awash in a flood of
clippings, fully apprised of Undine's appearances—nearly drown-
ing in them—but none the wiser about who his mother *is*. As he
repeats his father's mistake—that of seeking in Undine a substantial self that simply isn't there—we witness the ominous prophecy
of Ralph's sister coming true: "'He's going to be exactly like you,
Ralph—' she paused and then risked it: 'For his own sake, I wish
there were just a drop or two of Spragg in him'" (279). Is Undine flat,
or is she round? This distinction becomes meaningless in the face
of a character who has made the very question of interiority seem
so risibly beside the point.

As I have suggested, the novel draws out Undine's image to
gigantic dimensions as part of its larger attempt to demonstrate
the anti-liberal ruptures—between subjective and objective reality, truth and appearance, merit and success—characterizing the
turn of the twentieth century. As Susman puts it, "In the culture
of character, the public had insisted on some obvious correlation
between achievement and fame. Now that insistence is gone" (283).
But the most salient rupture of all in the novel—as this chapter has
tried to establish, my digression into celebrity notwithstanding—is

that between attainment and satisfaction. Undine's outstanding social advancement, her series of marriages, childbirth, entry into the ranks of European aristocracy—none of these momentous life events leaves even the slightest dent in Undine's prodigious appetite or has any enduring effect on her subjective life. According to the narrator, "She had everything she wanted, but she still felt, at times, that there were other things she might want if she knew about them" (362). If she cannot desire a definable object, she will desire to desire. And, in the novel's final scene, the perpetual desire presaged by this observation is shown to be more than merely speculation, as Undine finds a new position to covet. On discovering that a divorcée could not be an ambassador's wife, she concludes that that was "the one part she was really made for" (364).

In foreshadowing the perpetuity of Undine's desire, the ending clarifies one of the novel's most puzzling ambiguities. Because of the narrator's almost equal fascination with the business tycoon Elmer Moffatt, the husband with whom Undine ends the novel, it is tempting to interpret him as the solution to Undine's otherwise implacable desire, as Elaine Showalter and others have done.[15] Ralph and the rest of the old guard find something "heroic" and "Olympian" in Moffatt's battles with Wall Street; Ralph himself is so struck by Moffatt's perspicacity that he begins to suspect that "every financier" might be qualified to be a novelist. Moreover, Wharton's novel repeatedly draws parallels between Undine and the businessman. "Every Wall Street term had its equivalent in the language of Fifth Avenue," we are told (329). The desires of both accord with a sort of market calculus: She wants what others want, and he wants to procure what others will pay the most for. And, when she confides her conjugal woes to him near the end of the novel, Undine takes comfort in knowing that "here was some one who spoke her language, who knew her meanings, who understood instinctively all the deep-seated wants for which her acquired vocabulary had no terms" (328–29).

Kindred though this pair may seem, Wharton ultimately distinguishes them and intimates the reason why she, and not he, lays sole claim to the initials U. S. Though the era's corporate men differ from their nineteenth-century forebears in key respects, they are equally purposeful. These new men do not want the same things that the liberal individual wanted, but they, unlike Undine, want *something*, have an identifiable object for which they strive. The community-making "relative values" to which both of Undine's ex-husbands refer find their equivalent in the capitalist's exaltation of profit and business. Explaining to a bemused Undine why Raymond de Chelles will not sell his heirloom tapestries despite his financial straits, Moffatt declares, "His ancestors are *his* business: Wall Street's mine" (351). (However, as chapter 4 demonstrates at length, this aspect of businessmen in fiction eventually shifts.)

All men, in Moffatt's eyes, are guided by their attachment to some kind of "business." This sentiment dovetails with Charles Bowen's condemnation of American civilization earlier in the novel, which bears a striking resemblance to the analysis offered by Wharton's anonymous reviewer (quoted in the previous chapter). "In America," Bowen asserts, "the real *crime passionel* is a 'big steal,'" anticipating the reviewer's indictment of the American man's obsession with business (126). For Bowen and the reviewer alike, the Undines of America embody more fully than their male counterparts the shifts in modern society—are, in Bowen's words, the "monstrously perfect result of the system" (127). According to the reviewer, the promiscuity of their desires—in contrast to the single-mindedness of men—results from their adaptability, their stronger capacity to adjust to the nation's rapid ascent into abundance. As Wharton construes it, men in general—not just more conspicuous relics such as Ralph—have not yet managed to make the full transition into the consumption-oriented world of insatiability where women stand in waiting, "lonely and rather dizzy."

Thus, while Moffatt seems content to live happily ever after in a massive, gilded domesticity, Undine—like her sisters, Carrie and Selma—demonstrates that her own "business" will continue to consist in being dissatisfied, in proliferating desire. As social selves driven by the demands of an ever-changing social world, they cannot do otherwise. Dreiser's, Grant's, and Wharton's novels, as we have seen, imagine what Chopin could not: a new, viable form of female subjectivity that corresponded to the realities of a world ordered by consumerism and corporate commerce. In the process, they force the novel beyond the boundaries of classical literary realism, establishing perpetual dissatisfaction and open-endedness as hallmarks of the modern novel. The next chapter examines the effect of this tendency in early-twentieth-century American letters on the genre of fictional life writing. Whereas Dreiser and Wharton address themselves to the question of what the cultural shifts at the turn of the century might mean for conceptions of the self, the novelists in the following chapter take the next logical step, asking what all this might mean for conceptions of life—of the self as it extends through time.

CHAPTER THREE

The Bildungsroman after Individualism

Herrick and Glasgow

It has proven very difficult for scholars to contemplate the Bildungs-roman without the backdrop of classical liberalism. Associating it with the rise of the bourgeoisie, critics have traditionally located the subgenre's heyday in the nineteenth century and seen its plot to consist in a middle-class, usually male protagonist's self-directed attainment of a stable social identity. Once the protagonist achieves this identity, the desire driving his plot is extinguished, he is satisfied, and the novel ends.

Without denying this pattern's prevalence in depictions of modern life in the nineteenth century, I want, in this chapter, to demonstrate one way the subgenre shifted to accommodate the advent of consumer capitalism at the turn of the twentieth century. As its title suggests, Robert Herrick's scarcely discussed novel *One Woman's Life* (1913) depicts the life of an early-twentieth-century heroine. But, though intended to be representative of modern life in the United States ("Many hundreds of thousands, men and women, were weaving similar webs," notes the narrator [69]), the story of Milly Ridge's life does not resemble the individualist Bildungs-romane that predominate in earlier representations of modernity. Neither does the protagonist's life narrative in Ellen Glasgow's 1925 novel *Barren Ground*. Rather than offering closure for its heroine, the novel pictures her life as perennially open-ended (the title of the novel's final section is, tellingly, "Life-Everlasting"). Both heroines resist, in different ways, the kind of satisfaction that gave closure to the archetypal protagonist of the classical Bildungsroman. As we shall see, this modification of the novelistic subject is extremely significant.

But does this fact render Herrick's and Glasgow's novels failures within the subgenre? According to the terms set forth by one influential critic, it does. In his study of the European Bildungsroman, Franco Moretti defines literary failure—albeit "sketchily," he admits—as "the sort of thing that occurs when a form deals with problems it is unable to solve" (243). Moretti takes as his prime example James Joyce's *Portrait of the Artist as a Young Man*, which he uses to suggest the impossibility of reproducing the classical Bildungsroman in the early-twentieth century, the age of modernism. Moretti contends that the nineteenth century prized adulthood for its promise of social integration and that the Bildungsroman remained a crucial instrument for propagating this cultural value. But World War I, he argues, eroded that faith in adulthood, replacing it with a valorization of youth and regression. To write a story of growing self-consciousness and maturation in an era obsessed with the unconscious and regression was, as *Portrait* is meant to show, a hopeless pursuit that could not help but give way to modernist experimentation (hence *Ulysses*).

This is surely a compelling explanation of the transformation of the Bildungsroman in the twentieth century. In a new time, it failed, and, observing this failure time and again, novelists sought techniques that better accorded with the spirit of their age. The one problem with this elegant solution is its presumption that the only shapes the Bildungsroman could take were its nineteenth-century forms. To conclude that the form and the problems of such novels as *Portrait* are not compatible presupposes that, if they were, the novels would resemble their nineteenth-century predecessors—the touchstones in comparison to which these later novels are judged failures. As Moretti sees it, were *Portrait*'s form and the problems it takes up compatible—were it a literary success—the novel would have ended with Stephen's epiphany and with his recognition of his vocation as an artist.

Such a perspective implicitly denies the possibility that the sub-genre could adapt to its time and confront new questions as the old ones grew stale or became obsolete. Formation might fail to occur or simply look different in twentieth-century literature, but that observation alone would not enable us to say, without being prescriptive, that the subgenre itself failed during this period. We would be safer to conclude simply that it acquired new conventions and, from there, attempt to figure out what they mean. (Paradoxi-cally, this is precisely the approach that Moretti takes throughout the rest of the book, as he moves across national literary traditions.)

To be clear, my disagreement with Moretti is not over *Portrait* per se. I am suggesting that twentieth-century deviations from the classical Bildungsroman can signify more than just the decline of a genre or subgenre. Although Moretti confines his study to Europe, the Bildungsroman was a form adapted by novelists all over the world to reflect the particular circumstances of their places and times. But, though these novels' distinctive qualities are the result of their peculiar historical conditions, these conditions alone are not enough to explain the significance of these features. To under-stand these divergent features, we must consider them within the formal history of the Bildungsroman. Placing these novels within a formal history would be no different from the way that we approach any art form. In English prosody, for instance, non-iambic meter is significant precisely because it is a deviation from the standard. If we do not consult preestablished standards, swerves in the his-tory of art remain meaningless since, to invoke Edith Wharton's quotation once again, "convention is the first necessity of all art" (*Writing of Fiction* 54).

Artistic swerves, as Moretti's conclusion might lead us to be-lieve, do not equate to failure, and I aim to approach Herrick's and Glasgow's novels with this redemptive insight in mind. Though my focus here is on an early-twentieth-century US adaptation of the Bildungsroman, the procedure I am suggesting for treating devia-tions within the subgenre applies wherever it has been adopted and reshaped. Fortunately, recent scholarship on postcolonial regions such as South Africa and India have exemplified this approach, examining adaptations of the novel of formation as generative di-vergences articulating the problems of their times and places.[1] Yet scholars have been far less attentive to US novels that transform the terms of formation established by English and Continental archetypes. Before my discussion turns to two such US novels, a brief explanation of the conventions of formation that they revise is in order.

The passage of a character from unstable, dynamic youth to relatively stable adulthood constitutes one of the most repeated plotlines in nineteenth-century fiction. In the narrative space between the poles of this plotline, individual formation was believed to unfold. In these novels, a successful navigation through the perils of youth assures the protagonist a stable place in the social world—or, what was for these novels the same thing, an identity. Enough ink has been spilt denying the existence of novels exemplifying all the characteristics attributed to the Bildungsroman (except as it figures in the work of other scholars).[2] But, though the idea of a pure Bildungsroman may be as illusory as the idea of purity in any literary genre, the fact that novels have constructed identity as something achieved through the accumulation of experiences—experiences that can be narrated as the causes effecting a discernible identity— is irrefutable.

As Marianne Hirsch observes of the classical Bildungsroman, it "is founded on the belief in progress and the coherence of self-hood" ("From Great Expectations" 297). The protagonist gains self-consciousness, social identity is established, self and world become one, the end—such is the order of the classical novel of formation. The subgenre flourished in this form in a burgeoning mercantilist society, in which a rising middle class staked its claim to political power on the autonomy of the self. But, as we saw earlier via James Livingston, the replacement of the small producer and of proprietary capitalism by corporate capitalism made the self-governing, self-possessed individual at the heart of the liberal imagination untenable. The corporatizing impulse reshaping the economic order transformed US culture, bringing about "the regress of self-sufficiency and the progress of association" (qtd. in Livingston, "War and the Intellectuals" 438).

In addition to the shifting notions of selfhood occasioned by corporatization, the massive expansion of the avenues open to women at the turn of the century further complicated novelists' ability to write modern women's lives as closed-ended narratives. Marriage, remarriage, Boston marriage, spinsterhood, divorce, career—all these paths were open to the era's middle-class women, and, indeed, most of them were explored by Herrick's and Glasgow's active heroines. The refusal of these novelists to designate any phase of their protagonists' lives the definitive culmination of their development— the point at which their life narratives can be said to end—produces an air of uncertainty in these novels. Unlike the nineteenth-century Bildungsroman, they cannot confidently narrate their protagonists' journeys to some predictable, culturally sanctioned endpoint (such as marriage); instead, the narrators proceed with virtually as little sense of what is to follow as the novels' characters.

Jennifer Fleissner's *Women, Compulsion, Modernity* links the flourishing of naturalist fiction to this same widespread uncertainty about women's destinies at the turn of the century. According to Fleissner, it manifests itself in naturalist novels' predilection for description over narration: Uncertain about the future of women (and, as a corollary, of American civilization in general), naturalist fiction fixates on the present, obsessively describing it in hopes that doing so will uncover some clue about what lies ahead. Unlike Fleissner's texts, however, *One Woman's Life* depends on narration to demonstrate its central problem—that the passage of time is no guarantor of fixed formation. In fact, Herrick explicitly distances his work from the hyper-descriptive tendencies of his contemporaries. When the narrator takes a break from narrating, it is only to announce that he will not overdescribe and to deprecate writers who do: "It is not worth while to go into the budgetary details of this particular matrimonial venture. Other story-tellers have done that with painful literalness, and nothing is drearier than the dead accounts of the butcher and baker, necessary as they are" (164).

As Susan Fraiman's *Unbecoming Women* reveals, a similar uncertainty influenced fictional depictions of women's lives at an earlier historical moment in England. Women's relationship to the classical Bildungsroman has long been understood as precarious. The subgenre's classical paradigm of formation—organic integration with the social world through finding a public vocation and founding a home—was so much at odds with the conditions of women's lives in the nineteenth century that it was hard to imagine a female-centered storyline that would accord with it. However, Fraiman understands much of the fiction written by and about British women in the Regency and Victorian eras to be centrally concerned with female development. In good poststructuralist fashion, Fraiman argues that the category of womanhood was so riven by contending meanings as to complicate any conception of a norm for female development. Thus, Fraiman seeks to shift "the usual questions—'How does the hero of this novel come of age? What are the stages that mark his passage to maturity?'—to 'What are the several developmental narratives at work in this novel and what can they tell us about competing ideologies of the feminine?'" (12).

In Herrick's and Glasgow's novels, however, this indeterminacy becomes not only more radical but also definitive of modernity. Whereas Fraiman's texts ask, "How does it look to become a woman?" (with the concomitant assumption that women will become *something*), Herrick's asks, "Is *becoming* even possible in the first place?" In posing this question, *One Woman's Life* impugns the individualistic construal of development as a closed-ended process leading one to self-governance and socialization. These novelists' decision to write narratives of modern life that center on exactly the opposite of the modern liberal subject—male, satiable, self-enclosed—implies their conviction that individualism had become an obsolete paradigm for this new stage of modernity.

As we shall see, these authors' distinctly nonindividualist renderings of selfhood defy the teleological, closure-oriented pattern of the nineteenth-century plot of socialization. Like Dreiser and Wharton (discussed in chapter 2), Herrick fashions his protagonist in accord with Mead's ever-mutable social self. For Milly Ridge, the world is not some stable entity with which she must achieve an enduring harmony; instead, it is dynamic, requiring an endless series of temporary equilibrations—not simply the one grand equilibration implied within the concept of socialization.

Glasgow, on the other hand, contravenes liberal individualism through a communitarian construal of selfhood that undermines liberalism's valorization of consent. In this construal (which I draw on the philosopher Alasdair MacIntyre to formulate), individuals are not born blank slates whose lives culminate in either an acceptance of social norms (what Moretti terms "legitimation" or "consent" [16]) or a rejection of them. Instead, people begin life already, in a sense, socialized—members of existing social communities with their own distinctive histories. The fact of social belonging is the "given" of one's life, not the outcome of one's choices. This inheritance of relations constitutes one's "moral starting point," dictating, regardless of the individual's will, the direction in which she must proceed in pursuit of the good life. Such a conception of the self effectively reverses the poles of the classical novel of formation, positioning social belonging as the actuating fact at the beginning of an open-ended, unceasing search for the good. Importantly, the good is not "something already adequately characterized" (like the values central to socialization) but an unknown that we asymptotically approach over generations (if we're virtuous): "The good life for man is the life spent in seeking for the good life for man" (MacIntyre 219). It follows that, for MacIntyre, any life oriented toward the achievement of some fixed set of virtues (such as the individualist lives narrated in the pages of nineteenth-century fiction) would be misguided.

In different ways, these texts both demonstrate how US novelists appropriated the subgenre of the Bildungsroman to express the differences between their conception of selfhood and selfhood as it was conceived in the world of classical liberalism. Reading in tandem these two very different postindividualist adaptations of the classical Bildungsroman—one showing how development looks for the anchorless Meadian social self at the center of the previous chapter, the other exploring the ethical affordances of an associational age—provides a sense of the range of creative possibilities opened up by the decline of liberal individualism.

ROBERT HERRICK'S *ONE WOMAN'S LIFE*

Published the same year as Edith Wharton's *The Custom of the Country*, *One Woman's Life* shares with Wharton's better-remembered novel a desire to examine twentieth-century life as it was experienced by a new generation of American women. About this intention in his work, Herrick was quite explicit (and not just *One Woman's Life*), remarking in his memoirs his aim "to show incidentally through them [i.e., women] why the world is today what it seemed to be" (qtd. in Nevius 180). The novel narrates the life of the ambitious Milly Ridge from age sixteen into her late thirties, an interval during which she enters into a conventional marriage, motherhood, widowhood, a brief Boston marriage, and a second conventional marriage that may or may not last. (On Milly's fate, the novel's final lines are irresolute: She "was settled at last and, let us assume, 'lived happily ever after.'")

As one contemporary reviewer claims, likening Wharton's novel to Herrick's, Milly exemplifies the "spending woman" who had become "one of the stock figures of the newer fiction" (rev. of *Custom* 201). Despite her stockness, this figure clearly fascinated Herrick. Describing his protagonist's lifelong outrage at the dinginess of her family's first Chicago home, for instance, the narrator pauses in awe of Milly's uncommon faculties of discernment "But how did Milly Ridge at sixteen perceive all this?" he wonders (9). "What gave her the sense of social distinctions,—of place and condition,—at her age, with her limited, even if much-travelled experience of American cities?" He makes clear that understanding Milly's keen social sensitivity is no trivial matter, asserting that "to read this mystery will be to understand Milly Ridge—and something of America as well."

In telling the story of Milly Ridge, Herrick sees himself as filling the role for turn-of-the-century America that he believed realist novelists such as Thackeray filled for Victorian England—that of "social historian" (Herrick qtd. in Nevius 176). In so doing, he assumes the task of treating "the larger phenomena of our common life" with the precision of the sociologist. The fact that "our common life" should be, in Herrick's view, most legible through one woman's life is worth note. In true realist fashion, Herrick depends chiefly upon social types rather than hyper-particularized Jamesian individuals. As his remarks about Milly suggest, some types are more representative of an era than others. Some lives are more intensely the products of and thus better reflect the particular historical conditions shaping a society at a given time.

That "the spending woman" was the most apt figure for representing the changes in American society was not, however, always clear to Herrick. In an earlier novel, for example, Herrick surveys the American scene through thinking about the American couple. Nearly six hundred pages long, his 1908 novel *Together* is, in its sprawling ambition for comprehensiveness, among his most Thackerayan books. It features an array of couples—some wealthier than others but most belonging to the comfortable class—who operate, in effect, as the novel's characters. The very first sentence, if not the title, signals that this is a novel about modern marriage: Isabelle—who forms part of the protagonist couple—"stood before the minister who was to marry them, very tall and straight" (3). Here we are faced with what is probably the most modern dimension of this, as I'll show, mostly conservative novel, despite its scandalous (but profitable) reception:[3] It begins, rather than ends, in marriage, suggesting the possibility that wedlock may well not be the culmination of a woman's life, even if the novel ultimately undermines that possibility. On Isabelle's wedding day, the narrator identifies two possible paths for the marriage, through alluding to two of the women attending the wedding:

> Only two faces stood out from the others at this moment—the dark, mischievous face of Nancy Lawton, smiling sceptically. Her dark, little eyes seemed to say, "Oh, you don't know yet!" And the other was the large, placid face of a blond woman, older than the bride, standing beside a stolid man at the end of a pew. The serene, soft eyes of this woman were dim with tears, and a tender smile still lingered on her lips. She at least, Alice Johnston, the bride's cousin, could smile through the tears—a smile that told of the sweetness in life. . . . (7; ellipsis Herrick's)

As we saw in chapter 2 in examining *Sister Carrie*, this either-or dichotomy became a tactic for modern novelists to introduce a third way, one distinguishing the new times from the old. Just as Carrie defies the terms set for her—that, in going to the city, she'll either fall into "saving hands" and become better or assume the "cosmopolitan standard of virtue" and become worse (1)—so Isabelle and her husband, John Lane, defy the terms set for them. What are those terms? Unsurprisingly, as in Carrie's case, it's a Manichaean choice between extremes, angelic virtue or diabolical vice. Whereas the marriage of another couple, the Johnstons, is "perfection," that of "two who had lived together, body and soul" (571)—the Victorian ideal—the Lawtons' is marred by flagrant and serial infidelity. In typical realist fashion, the Lanes triumph through—forgive the pun, but it is Herrick's—taking the middle lane.

What is most interesting, for our purposes, is how they get there. For most of the novel, Isabelle is, to all appearances, exactly the kind of character we examined in chapter 2. For one, she is repeatedly depicted as insatiable, impelled by the same kind of objectless desire that we have seen elsewhere. In a characteristic moment detailing her longings, the narrator tells us, "As the woman stared down into the twilight, she seemed to see afar of what she had longed for, held out her hands towards,—life" (247). Like Grant's Selma White, she is obsessed with "development" yet has no concrete idea where that development should lead. Imbibing the discourse of "personality," "She meant to be Somebody" (310). A social self through and through, she is "an impressionable character in which the equilibrium is not found and fixed" (247). All signs point to Isabelle's joining the women of chapter 2 and breaking the couple structure holding *Together* together. And I mean that quite literally: By part 5 (of seven parts), Isabelle, bored with the taciturn but dutiful businessman she has married, is on the brink of leaving him for a more "interesting" writer type.

But, before things go too far, Herrick disciplines her, and in the most brutal fashion. Her brother—the dearest person in her life—sees what she is on the verge of doing, and, in his effort to save her, is shot dead by her would-be lover. Thus begins the rehabilitation of Isabelle. Shocked by the sudden loss of her brother, which she understands to be her fault, she visits her childhood friend Margaret in Vermont, in need of rest. Margaret, who herself has been unlucky in love, is boarding with the Shorts, a rustic couple described as "the marriage type of the pioneer,—a primitive, body-wracking struggle of two against all, a perfect type, elemental but whole" (513). Editorializing, as he is over-wont to do in this novel, Herrick continues, "And this remains the large pattern of marriage to-day wherever sound. Two bodies, two souls are united for the life struggle to wring order out of chaos,—physical and spiritual" (513). Inspired by the Shorts' example and chastened by her brother's sacrifice, Isabelle recommits herself to her husband, taking an active interest in his life, including his work; in turn, he shares more of his work with her—in fact, "liked to talk things over with her" (585). They move out west for "a new world, a new light, a new life," and, most importantly, are better together (595).

Predicated on the pervasive notion that the ills of modern American society have everything to do with the alienation of husband from wife, this happy ending is utterly contrived. It is Herrick at his most wishful and his least realistic, committing much the same error to which James admitted in having his millionaire protagonist in *The American* rejected by the broke French aristocrats (see chapter 4). The wishful, unrealistic quality of the novel was clear even to one of Herrick's friends, who told him so directly.[4] The undue length of this novel helps give Herrick away. Obviously, his strategy of making the couples serve the function of characters contributed to the excessive length, for doing so set him the task not only of making the couples distinct but also of making the characters within the couples distinct. In addition to this fact, though, the novel is overrun with editorial comment. In fact, as Blake Nevius observes, "in *Together*, notably, he stretched his prerogative to the limit" (175). The novel's "series of homilies and editorial digressions" seem telltale signs of an author insecure about the capacity of his story to speak for itself (Nevius 175). We have good reason to suspect that, in 1908, Herrick was still too stunned by the changing landscape to portray it dispassionately. In *Together*, we find the author giving us the America—and the American woman—he wants rather than the one staring him in the face.

Five years later, though, we have a different Herrick. It's no accident that Nevius is able to class *One Woman's Life* among Herrick's "more conventional realistic novels," in which "the comment is held to a minimum" (175). Here he is prepared to face the fact, no matter how much he may rue it, that the nineteenth century is over and that a new world order has been established. We see as much in his turn from Isabelle to Milly, who will not be chastened. And, in so turning, Herrick makes the full transition—half-enacted but ultimately abandoned in *Together*—into the current of modern American fiction.

Herrick's choice of Milly as his representative social type, the one through whom contemporary America could be best grasped, points to an important shift in conceptions of the modern subject. In the reissued edition of *The Way of the World*, defending his study's confinement to novels about white men, Moretti explains that, "for a long time, the west European middle-class man held a virtual monopoly on [wide cultural formation, professional mobility, and full social freedom], which made him a sort of structural *sine qua non* of the subgenre. Without him, and without the social privileges he enjoyed," Moretti continues, "the *Bildungsroman* was difficult to write, because it was difficult to imagine" (x). Herrick suggests that something had changed to make the lives of young middle-class women of the twentieth century the very thing that men's had been for the nineteenth-century novel: vehicles for figuring the shape of modernity.

This is not to suggest that Milly's life simply replicates the linear trajectory from adolescence to adulthood central to the male-dominated, nineteenth-century novel of formation. For there is no point at which Milly's narrative settles. Like many other heroines in twentieth-century American literature, she exemplifies the conception of the social self elaborated by Mead—one of Herrick's many pragmatist colleagues at the University of Chicago. In line with Mead's conception of the social self, Milly's life is an ongoing oscillation between subject and object that defies closure. As the quotation with which I began suggests, Milly possesses keen social instincts, able to sense instantly when she or anything pertaining to her is not or will not be met with approval. And the pursuit of approval is the driving force in her life, all her actions working in service of it. In the narrator's words, "This social passion . . . had been the dominant note of her life" (17). Episode after episode shows Milly fashioning her taste and behavior to accord with the varying preferences of her social environs. As she fastidiously directs the arrangement of their drab new Chicago home, the narrator notes, "Somewhere she had learned that the living room of a modern household was no longer called the 'parlor,' by those who knew, but the 'drawing-room,' and with the same unerring instinct she had discovered the ignominy of this early Victorian heritage" (10–11). And, naturally, these are the terms she adopts. Elsewhere, we hear her whine, "Oh, papa!," followed by the narrator's parenthetical comment, "Somewhere in the course of her wanderings Milly had learned not to say 'paw'" (14).

The language employed to characterize Milly's pursuit of approval, her "social passion," is crucial. It is not a conscious enterprise but an "instinct," something she can resist no more than hunger or thirst. The abstract nature of her desire and the semiconscious way in which it functions make it hard to state with any confidence what, exactly, she wants at any given moment (hence the tentativeness of the novel's final lines). No sooner does the narrator establish that "her ambition" was "to have 'some place for herself'" than he points out the referential instability of what Milly seeks: "What she meant by having a place for herself in the world she did not yet understand of course. Nor what she could do with it, having achieved it. It was an instinct, blind in the manner of instincts, of her dependent womanhood. She was quite sure that something must happen,—a something that would give her a horizon more spacious than that of the West Side" (16). We see the ephemerality of her desire once again in the semantically nimble phrase Herrick uses to characterize her aspirations—"the real, right thing." To explain her decision to break off her engagement to the ascetic Clarence Albert, for instance, she claims that she "couldn't—it wasn't the real, right thing" (109). Before marrying Jack Bragdon, for whom she jilts Clarence, Milly concludes in frustration that "it was useless to explain to her father and her grandmother the imperious call of 'the real, right thing'..." (148). Despite her passionate insistence upon it, "the real, right thing" never seems to refer to the same thing. Milly's aimless drive ensures that she will continue to strive, continue to chase in vain that chimera called satisfaction.

The social self—an endlessly desirous and endlessly mutable entity—is fundamentally incompatible with any notion of perdurable satisfaction, the decisive condition that brought the classical novel of formation to its harmonious halt.[5] "The novel of formation's plot is," according to Hirsch, "a version of the quest story" (297). But the problem here is that there is no equivalent quest-terminating Holy Grail. As long as there are new things to want and new people to please—as there always will be in the dynamic, consumption-ridden world Milly inhabits—her life will continue to defy the kind of object-oriented, stabilizing quest form that structured the lives of her fictional predecessors and the imagined life of the liberal individual.

To show that Milly's life is incompatible with this trajectory, Herrick embeds within her story compactly narrated renderings of lives that are. The neat manner in which the narrator chronicles the formation of these characters—providing them clear beginnings, middles, and ends—contrasts so starkly with the approach to Milly's life as to make her seem an altogether different species of human. This contrast is enhanced by the inclusion of *one* in the novel's title, which distinguishes the protagonist even while the novel insists on her representativeness. On the one hand, this paradox, in which Milly is both distinctive and typical, is redolent of the "obvious difficulty" that Warren Susman identifies at the heart of the culture of personality: "One is to be unique, be distinctive, follow one's feelings, make oneself stand out from the crowd, and at the same time appeal—by fascination, magnetism, attractiveness to it" (280). On the other, it is an attempt to show that her kind of subject exists among other kinds but that hers is the most representative, the most modern. Her life acts as a metonym for the legions of other modern female lives that owe their existence to a new cultural order.

The first life from which hers is distinguished, that of her deceased mother, serves to establish Milly as rootless and her mother's rootedness as old-fashioned. Milly's mother is of an aristocratic Kentucky family and depicted as a dainty relic from the romanticized South. Milly's father's search for work forces the Ridge family to relocate constantly, and her mother is described as having "gradually succumbed under the perpetual tearing up of her thin roots, and finally faded away altogether in the light housekeeping phase of their existence in St. Louis" (6).

In contrast, Milly thrives throughout their peripatetic roving: "Everywhere the family had put foot to earth in its wanderings, Milly had acquired friends easily,—at school, in church, among the neighbors,—what chance afforded from the mass" (17). But it would be wrong to construe Milly's forging of "friendships" as the creation of long-lasting bonds that situate her in a permanent set of relations (such as the kind whose absence so distresses Mrs. Ridge). Upon leaving each city, seen off at the train station by her many adoring friends, Milly "kissed them all, and swore to each that she would write, which she promptly forgot to do." "But," the narrator ironically reassures us, "she loved them all, just the same" (18).

Milly's inability to form the enduring ties so vital to her mother is an important aspect of her constitution as a social self. To form permanent attachments would require some kind of subjective anchor, an unchanging core on to which things, persons, and ideas could latch. But, as we have seen via Mead, the only thing that does not change about the social self is that it is always changing: "The inner response to our reaction to others is . . . as varied as is our social environment" (482). An unyielding attachment to preferences and lifestyles across varying social milieux would suggest an unbreakable continuity of self immune to the vicissitudes of the social world. The narrator repeatedly makes clear that Milly's preferences and comportment resist taking such a rigid form, perhaps most succinctly in the description of her experience at finishing school. Her attempt to "finish herself" (a phrase the narrator encloses in scare quotes) comes to naught because "learning passed over Milly like a summer sea over a shining sandbar and left no trace behind, none whatever" (31). The very suggestion that such a person as Milly Ridge could be "finished"—could ever cast roots in the customs and preferences of some fixed milieu—seems preposterous to the narrator.

Like her mother's staid Southern aristocratic heritage, the ascetic Puritanism of her father's line serves as another contrastive element in Herrick's attempt to characterize Milly. This contrast is most manifest in Grandma Ridge, who "embodied unpleasant duties" and "was a vessel of unwelcome reproof that could be counted upon to spill over at raw moments" (7). The narrator takes pains to distinguish Milly from this unalterably finished portrait of Victorian probity: "Wherever she [Milly] derived this social passion," the narrator notes, it was "obviously not from Grandma Ridge" (17). A native of the fabricated, obviously Protestant middle-class town of Euston, Pennsylvania, Grandma Ridge values prudence and moderation above all and, accordingly, is constantly chiding her consumption-obsessed granddaughter. When, for instance, Milly begs for the chance to throw a party, Mrs. Ridge "observed coldly," "It would be a great extravagance" (79). She had heard that "tiresome word," *extravagance*, so frequently from her grandmother that she "came to loathe it most of all the words in the language."

Their differences come into clearest view when Milly impetuously breaks her engagement to the man whom the novel figures as Grandma Ridge's younger male doppelgänger. Descended from a long line of respectable New Englanders, Clarence Albert "always counted his change carefully, like a good puritan" (101). Against Milly's profligate entreaties to erect a grand home before the wedding, "Clarence Albert, like a prudent mariner of the puritan type, dwelt upon the signs of dire storm, and counselled their not building for the present" (105). The novel is unambiguous in its aim to have us see this circumspect bachelor and Grandma Ridge as cut from the same cloth, as two of the same social type: "The old lady approved of Clarence Albert. They discussed religion together. They had the same Victorian standards and principles about life" (103). The narrator is careful to show that their similar traits stem from their comparable cultural backgrounds. The pair is not just parsimonious but *puritanically* so; their "standards and principles about life" are not just conservative but "Victorian." This mode of characterization forces us to construe Milly's clashes with them not as incidental interpersonal disagreements but as the larger expression of sociological differences within turn-of-the-century US society.

Distinguishing Milly from this particular social type—the austere Protestant respected for exemplifying a set of socially sanctioned virtues—is part of the novel's strategy to locate Milly's modernity in her love for consumption and her astounding social adaptability. In language almost identical to his, the novel dramatizes the historical shift from character to personality that Susman describes in his discussion of turn-of-the-century US culture. The "culture of character," Susman explains, dominated the eighteenth and nineteenth centuries, periods of comparative scarcity and nation building. It emphasized duty, strong work ethic, conformity, and self-sacrifice—all, significantly, virtues required for the socialization of the archetypal protagonist of the classical novel of formation. In the more prosperous twentieth century, however, the onset of consumer culture ushered in the "culture of personality," an era when self-sacrifice gave way to self-gratification, probity to congeniality.

Susman detects this cultural shift in the lexical transformations within mainstream discourse, and these transformations are vital to the novel's depiction of Milly. In place of the character-oriented adjectives suffusing Herrick's descriptions of Grandma Ridge and Clarence Albert, the novel uses the register of personality to characterize Milly. *Fascinating, stunning, magnetic, attractive, glowing*—these are the terms that order social life in the age of personality and the ones repeatedly used to describe this protagonist. After the first party Milly hosts in Chicago, for instance, Mrs. Bowman—"the leader of our most exclusive circle"—declares, "She has a very magnetic personality, your young friend . . . A magnetic personality—it's all in that" (83). What seems even more striking is Herrick's acute awareness of the historical significance of Mrs. Bowman's diction. "The phrase had not become meaningless then," the narrator notes, "and it aptly described Milly's peculiar power. . . . It is a power much desired in democratic societies, where all must be done by the individual of his own initiative—a power independent of birth, education, money,—with a touch of the mystery of genius in it, of course" (83). Here Herrick appears to go one step farther than Susman does: Recalling Livingston's conjunction of pragmatism with democracy, he links personality not only to a later stage of modernity but also specifically to the "democratic" United States (which seem to be one and the same in Herrick's imagination).

This linkage imparts a new valence to the fact that Grandma Ridge and Clarence Albert are "Victorian." Their old-fashioned tendencies take the shape of foreignisms, throwing into relief Herrick's equation of the United States with modernity. In this novel, to be truly American is to be modern, and to be truly modern is to be American. In the same vein, the narrator tells us that Grandma Ridge is what her generation "described as 'ladylike'"—a descriptor highlighting her un-Americanness and undemocratically placing her merit in her performance of rank. But Milly's merit lies in being a woman rather than a lady: "The secret of Milly's hold upon all her women friends: they felt the woman in her, the pure character of their sex more highly expressed in her than in any one else they knew. She was the unconscious champion of their hearts" (158).

Mrs. Ridge, the Southern belle, and the Puritan pair of Grandma Ridge and Clarence Albert are all regionally defined relics of a bygone era. Their predictable, familiar lives unfit them for the center stage of Herrick's depiction of a specifically American modernity. They are useful only insofar as they help distinguish Milly. Similarly, Herrick introduces the butch Ernestine Geyer, whose life story is compactly narrated in a nine-page chapter called "The

New Woman," to underscore the modernity, the up-to-dateness, of his Milly Ridge. As Ernestine is meant to show, though Milly is unmistakably a product of modern times, we would err in viewing her as a version of the economically independent New Woman that had come into being some decades earlier. (Far from the self-supporting New Woman, Milly is "a fortuitous, somewhat parasitic creature"—or, in "Ernestine's more vulgar idiom," "'a little grafter'" [404].) In the end—largely thanks to the narrator's great efforts at masculinizing her—Ernestine turns out to be little more than another of the many old-fashioned men who fuel Milly's spending.

Ernestine's life story is worth recounting, for its simplicity and narratability set her apart from Milly. Born in St. Louis, Ernestine moved with her family to New York at a very young age. At fourteen, she left school and went to work, as was common (a "coming of age") for young women of her class. The narrator speculates that she "would probably have turned out, as most of her kind turn out, either have become the wife of a workingman with a brood of children to feed ... or gone to her end more rapidly on the streets" (313). But a terrible accident at the laundry where she worked scalded her severely, leaving her with an unattractive scar on one side of her body and a withered limb for a right arm. Concluding that "no man would ever think of marrying her," Ernestine threw all her energy into work and eventually became "indispensable" to the establishment (313). Over the years, her salary continued to grow (at the time she meets Milly, she is earning five thousand a year, merely one thousand less than Milly's deceased husband made). And, despite one unfortunate dalliance—with a gold-digger out to exploit her—Ernestine remains unwed, living vicariously through her neighbors, whose snug domesticity she stalks like a benign Grendel.

This neat sequence of events is what has made Ernestine into an independent, hardened, unfeminine—in a word "New"—woman. Yet a life of loneliness has left an affective void that she yearns to fill. Though she may have turned her back on men, it is clear that Ernestine has not given up on domesticity or, as remains implicit but conspicuous enough, on romantic love. In the Boston marriage he depicts—concentrated mainly in a chapter titled "Milly's New Marriage"—Herrick veers much closer to lesbianism than Henry

James dared nearly thirty years earlier. Not only is Ernestine frequently referred to as a man ("Mr. Geyer," the "Laundry-man," "one first-class man") and called "queer"; the novel also occasionally figures her, Milly, and Milly's daughter as a heterosexual family, mapping the relationships constituting the bourgeois home onto this trio. Young Virginia sums up the configuration best. After Ernestine declares one night at table, "We make a pretty cosey family," Virgie adds, "Mamma, pap, daughter," "pointing demurely to Ernestine as 'Papa'" (329). Ernestine's "robust, confident manner cheered Milly as much as her embrace. She trusted Ernestine's strength as she had once that of her husband" (331).

Reproducing bourgeois domesticity—a form of affiliation as familiar to Herrick's readers as the blue sky—this homosocial (homosexual?) arrangement does not comprise the "flexible and shifting roles" that Kate McCullough finds in Sarah Orne Jewett's more oblique depiction of a Boston marriage (57). Herrick's decision to present the otherwise unorthodox alliance in the conjugal terms that his readers would recognize seems consonant with his attempt to represent it as a union no less capable of fulfilling Milly than her heterosexual marriage had been. In fact, their arrangement works so well that, on seeing the two women together, one of Milly's acquaintances is moved to wonder why "more women don't do the same thing" (340). He continues, "Now Ernestine has every good quality of a man, and she can't deceive you with a chorus girl! It cuts out all the sex business, which is a horrid nuisance—see the newspapers." The Boston marriage seems to have everything that the conventional heterosexual marriage has, and more.

Unsurprisingly, this 1913 novel does not vouchsafe whether these two women ever consummate their relationship, notwithstanding the presumptuous comments of Milly's garrulous male friend. But it is suggestive enough to persuade us to view this arrangement as more than platonic, especially if we accept Lillian Faderman's nonsexual definition of lesbianism.[6] The Boston marriage is just another one of Herrick's exhaustive measures to cover all bases in his attempt to establish once and for all that Milly is insatiable, incapable of reaching closure of any kind (to whose appeal not even his putative New Woman, Ernestine, is immune). Valerie Rohy suggests that American literature figures lesbianism as a representational problem, an "impossibility" that works to naturalize heterosexual coupling.[7] But Herrick's unsubtle depiction of this "New Marriage" evinces no more representational difficulty than his depiction of Milly's heterosexual relationships. Representing lesbianism isn't the problem for Herrick; imagining satisfaction for his heroine—that's the real impossibility. Love of no kind will settle her. Moreover, through his incorporation of Ernestine, Herrick seems to anticipate readers' temptations to view the widowed Milly as a representative of New Womanhood, a somewhat recently emerged social category in the Anglo-American world who, at one point, embodied the modern developments of the time. But, as we shall see, even this identity was, by 1913, too outmoded for the likes of Milly.[8]

"And so, to sum it up in conventional terms," the narrator teasingly announces, bringing old literary conventions to bear on this unconventional union, "one might call Milly's new marriage a success and expect that the modest little household of 'number 236' would go its peaceful way uneventfully to nature's fulfilment of a comfortable middle age—and thus interest us no more" (344). Though her choice of partner would seem unorthodox, to conclude Milly's plot at this point would formally align it with the classical Bildungsroman. After a formative period of youth (such as that experienced by Ernestine and more meanderingly by the mutable Milly), the pair, according to this well-worn literary blueprint, would settle into a cozy, unvarying midlife. "For a time both Ernestine and Milly so believed it would be. But they were deceived. Human affairs, even of the humblest, rarely arrange themselves thus easily and logically" (344). While taking a moment to sneer at the neatness of old realist conventions, Herrick again reminds us that the modern, exemplary life of his protagonist resists to its core the closure-oriented trajectories of Victorian fiction. Unlike Ernestine's, Milly's selfhood defies neat narration, culminating neither in spinsterhood nor in consummating (even if unconventional) wedlock, the two decisive fates before her New Woman companion.[9]

Just as all seems settled, Milly grows restless. Concerned that her life lacks "meaning," Milly yearns to do something that will leave a mark on the world (365). Yet Herrick slyly turns even this existential crisis into a bid for social approval, transforming this introspective unrest into the product of Milly's other-directed social selfhood: "Like all poor mortals who have not either triumphed indubitably in the world's eyes or sunk irretrievably into the mire, she hungered for some definite self-accomplishment, something that would give meaning and dignity to her own little life" (365). Milly's sense of failure, Herrick suggests, is born of the act of viewing herself through "the world's eyes."[10]

Milly seeks to find this sense of "definite self-accomplishment" in the establishment of her own pastry shop, after the fashion of the ones she had admired in Paris. Misguidedly believing that their union is for Milly all that it is for her—the crown of middle age— Ernestine willingly offers to pour her life's savings into the endeavor, happy to help the woman with whom she plans to spend the rest of her life. "She would have slaved for her cheerfully all her life and felt it a privilege," the narrator notes (405). Little does she know that it is fear of the onset of stability that has set Milly into motion: "Now Milly was drifting towards that dead sea of purposeless middle age, and instinctively feared her fate" (345).

To make a long story short, they move to Chicago and establish the pastry shop, it ultimately fails, and Milly abandons Ernestine for an old flame. In the final moments of the novel, we find Milly preparing to set off with her new fiancé to California, then conceived of as "a strange new land" (402). The mystery and open-endedness of her impending journey mirror the indeterminacy of her life, as it has always been and as it always will be. An "adventuress," she is the full embodiment of her age—like Wharton's Undine Spragg, precisely "what civilization had made of her" (404).[11] For Milly, there is no end, only new beginnings, as her figurative response to the optimistic injunction to "go west" would imply. Fittingly, the novel concludes with a decisive ending not for Milly but for one of the many closure-oriented social types that both she and modernity have left behind: Ernestine, the New Woman. What will become of Milly, we do not know: She "was settled at last and, let us assume, 'lived happily ever after'"—the "let us assume" and scare quotes undermining any suggestion of closure (405). Yet we know exactly what lies ahead for the heartbroken Ernestine: "The new woman plodded sturdily through the mucky Chicago streets on her way to the eternal Job" (405).

As Milly's story demonstrates, writing the life history of the other-directed self that Herrick and others imagined to constitute modern subjectivity required replacing closed-ended narratives of socialization with open-ended stories that leave room for endless desire and its concomitant ontological flux. Yet, interestingly, as we shall see in Glasgow's *Barren Ground*, even novelists who did not understand modern subjectivity in Mead's terms were rejecting the individualist, closure-oriented plots of nineteenth-century realist fiction. Like Herrick, Glasgow found it unrealistic to imagine modern women's lives as a closed-ended process terminated by the extinction of desire—what Herrick refers to as "nature's fulfilment of a comfortable middle age." Yet, although Glasgow also construes selfhood as permeable and the product of social relations, her view of relatedness diverges drastically from Herrick's.

ELLEN GLASGOW'S *BARREN GROUND*

Ellen Glasgow's 1925 *Barren Ground* contributes to her generation's effort to redefine modern subjectivity in a postindividualist, corporate era but with a difference: She brings to the enterprise an ethical commitment that transforms it into a communitarian, rather than merely community-oriented, affair. This undertaking compels Glasgow's novel to *think* very differently from previous realist novels. As Nancy Armstrong has shown, in the eighteenth and nineteenth centuries—the heyday of liberal individualism—"novels think like individuals about the difficulties of fulfilling oneself as an individual under specific cultural historical conditions" (*How Novels Think* 10). The novel ingenuously tells two stories: On the one hand, it narrates the long, never-ending development of its heroine; on the other, the novel offers a metanarrative of its own genesis, a journey in which it confronts and ultimately transcends older conventions of realist fiction. In other words, *Barren Ground* is as much a realist story of personal formation as it is the story of the realist novel's *re*-formation.

In seeking to understand *Barren Ground* in relation to the history of the Bildungsroman, a common mode of the realist novel, I depart very deliberately from scholars who classify Glasgow's novel as naturalist. For instance, in the essay "'Where Are the

Ladies?,'" which argues for the prominence of women in naturalism—a literary movement frequently associated with men and
masculinity—Donna Campbell suggests that Glasgow's novel belongs to naturalism for its linking together of "labor, sexuality, and
maternity" (165) and its "epiphanies about the brutal nature of the
world" (162). Jennifer Travis claims that *Barren Ground* is "a naturalist novel to its core" for many of the same reasons (396).

Basing their classifications more on thematic content than on
style, such studies neglect one of naturalism's defining features:
its tendency to describe at the expense of narration what Fleissner has characterized as the genre's "stuckness in place" (*Women,
Compulsion, Modernity* 8–9). Narrating roughly three decades of
its protagonist's life, *Barren Ground* is hardly stuck; with its central
focus on formation, it—like all the novels discussed in my study—
simply cannot afford to be. Furthermore, Glasgow referred to her
work—and not just *Barren Ground*—as "social history," aligning her
novels with the sociological, often ethnographic function associated with realist fiction.[12] Finally, classifying the novel as naturalist
risks obscuring its profoundly transnational and transhistorical
vision. As I mention earlier, Glasgow always understood herself as
working within a long tradition of realist writing that included both
American and foreign masters. In *A Certain Measure*, a collection of
Glasgow's critical essays on fiction, she writes,

> From those explorers of the heart, the true realists, I learned also, if
> I had not already perceived this elementary principle in the canons
> of art, that a universe of ideas divides the novel bearing a sincere
> emotion toward life from the novel that depends upon a sterile con-
> vention. (17)

Barren Ground shows Glasgow grappling with her realist inheritance. The novel progresses through multiple phases in the history
of realist writing, rejecting each in its turn as an inadequate mode
for representing the life of its modern heroine. It enacts its revision
in three stages, stages mirrored in the novel's tripartite organization, with a tidiness that makes H. L. Mencken's description of the
novel as "competently planned" seem stingy (259). Each of the three
parts is titled after a plant that emblematizes its subject matter,

and each corresponds to a stage in the protagonist's and the novel's development. The first two parts, "Broomsedge" and "Pine," show Glasgow trying out but finally repudiating two past modes for representing women in Anglo-American fiction. In the final section, "Life-Everlasting," Glasgow discovers a fresh alternative for her heroine, one that avails itself of the ethical possibilities opened up by the shift from liberal individualism to a "corporate" paradigm in American culture.

Glasgow's preface conveys some sense of her revisionary intent. After noting her high estimate of the novel—"If I might select one of my books for the double-edged blessing of immortality," she claims, "that book would be, I think, *Barren Ground*"—she explains her wish to "write of the South not sentimentally, as a conquered province, but dispassionately, as a part of the larger world," to "write not of Southern characteristics, but of human nature" (vii). Significantly, Glasgow sees her heroine as "universal," existing "wherever a human being has learned to live without joy, wherever the spirit of fortitude has triumphed over the sense of futility" (viii). In so conceiving of the novel, Glasgow aligns her goals not only with realist aims (hence the explicit renunciation of sentimentalism in favor of dispassionate objectivity) but also with those at the heart of the classical Bildungsroman. The "final appeal [of the] *Bildungsroman*," according to Jerome H. Buckley, "lies in the author's capacity to make his [protagonist's] development seem representative as well as idiosyncratic" (7). Whatever Dorinda Oakley's idiosyncrasies and however much she is the product of the author's fancy ("She had been close to me for ten years before I began her story," writes Glasgow), she is meant to be exemplary (viii).

As we have seen, the classical Bildungsroman took white men as its exemplary subjects, and Glasgow is clearly signaling her departure. In insisting on the representativeness of her heroine, Glasgow is, of course, voicing a belief quite common in early-twentieth-century American society, even if not in existing examples of the novel of formation. We know that many during the time thought that women represented the modernizing forces of the era far better than men did. This assumption was predicated largely on the celerity with which middle-class women's lives had changed between the nineteenth and twentieth centuries. Transformed seemingly overnight in the culture's imagination from passionless stewards of the private sphere into avid consumers and wage earners, women appeared to embody the dynamism and unpredictability of modern society. (This is why in *The Education of Henry Adams* the eponymous author invokes the figure of "the Dynamo" in contemplating modern woman.) Fleissner has shown that modern woman's unprecedented mutability gave rise to a widespread uncertainty about her future—uncertainty that translated for many, including some of the nation's leaders, into anxiety. I think that it's just as reasonable to suggest that this uncertainty also, like the decline of liberal individualism, created imaginative space for artists to explore new ways of ordering the social world. It provided an irresistible blank canvas for novelistic experimentation. With modern woman's future yet unwritten, the novelist was free to write it. What better, more ambitious channel through which to do so than the Bildungsroman, a subgenre distinctly interested in imagining entire life trajectories?

The imaginative appeal of open-ended futures is likely part, though not all, of what inspired the second major generic deviation advertised in Glasgow's preface: its rural setting. In the traditional Bildungsroman, to achieve representativeness, the protagonist must exchange his provincialism for cosmopolitanism by making a life for himself in the city. The multifarious city, treated as a microcosm of the wide world, provides the mettle-testing experiences that guide him to maturity. In contrast, Glasgow would have us see the rural South as "part of the larger world," as a site just as rich as any urban center. However, like the era's modern woman, its richness for this novelist (unlike the sentimental Southern writers whom Glasgow criticizes) lies not in its substantive qualities but in its indeterminacy—or, rather, the potential immanent in that indeterminacy. Moreover, as we shall see, Glasgow reverses the classical novel of formation's valuations of rural and urban spaces: Dorinda's short time in the city functions not as the training ground for real life but as a respite from it—a never-never land where she can defer the vexing questions of adulthood indefinitely.

Broomsedge: The Nineteenth-Century Marriage Plot

Named after the weed that covers Pedlar's Mill in a drab uniformity, the first part of the novel is concerned with the stultifying effects of hackneyed conventions on both its heroine and literature. Here we find Dorinda seeking the meaning of life where scores of heroines before her have found it—in love and marriage. "At twenty," the narrator explains, presuming upon our expectations for young heroines, "her imagination was enkindled by the ardour that makes a woman fall in love with religion or an idea" (12). Viewing the attainment of love as "the end of all striving for her healthy nerves, her vigorous youth, the crown and the fulfillment of life" (59), she stakes all her happiness on Jason Greylock, who, having studied medicine in New York, is the town's closest thing to a young gentleman.

Significantly, in describing Dorinda's perspective during her infatuation with Jason, the narrator makes use of distinctively Flaubertian techniques of obliquity and tinting to signal the judgment-impairing effects of romance. During the months of courtship, "while her eyes were full of dreams," there was "a richer gloss on her hair, which was blue black in the shadow" (109). This, along with the "thin blue light [that] wavered and vanished again," recalls the famous "blue veil" behind which Emma Bovary views the world. Repeatedly, Dorinda is depicted as shrouded: the blue gloss on her hair, the "velvet softness to her body," "her warmer flush," the reference to a "natural Dorinda" who "still survived beneath" (109). It is as if romance has formed a gauzy but airtight barrier between her and reality.

Much like Charles Bovary, Jason Greylock is not immune to the deceptions of romance. Emboldened by the passion of the moment, Jason impulsively declares, "What I ought to do is . . . marry you today" (116). But the sobering influence of reality (the reality of his obligation to another woman of a more powerful family and the risks that crossing her would involve) deflates him: "'That's what I'd like to do,' he said slowly, while his rosy visions were obliterated by the first impact with reality" (116). Romance and reality are constantly clashing, each throwing the other into fuller relief. As we have witnessed, romance is depicted as the coloring or defocusing of reality. Thus, at the moment when reality asserts itself inexorably—when, that is, Dorinda sees Jason and Geneva Ellgood return to Pedlar's Mill as husband and wife—the haze and tint instantly dissipate: "Clear and sharp, she saw him with the vividness of a flash of lightning, and beside him, she saw the prim, girlish figure of Geneva Ellgood" (154).

At this critical juncture, as she lies prostrate in the mud—pregnant, abandoned, and worn down by the storm—Dorinda and the novel are faced with a momentous decision. They can submit to the conventions of romance's dark underside, the seduction narrative, or they can pull themselves up from the abjection of a failed love story and explore new paths—in Dorinda's case, toward a life not constrained by romance and, in the novel's, toward new formal possibilities. To do the former would be to accept the terms of maturity set forth by the traditional realist novel. As we have seen, the classical Bildungsroman equates maturity with socialization, a process entailing the protagonist's internalization of prevailing social values. For Dorinda, as for her Victorian predecessors, to internalize her community's values would entail accepting demise as her just deserts. It would oblige her, in short, to lie down and perish in her ready-made grave of wood mold.

Rejecting these outmoded constraints altogether, however, Dorinda gets up, and the novel goes on. In defiance of a long history of novels centering on female protagonists, Dorinda concludes that real life is not reducible to love. To underscore this point, Glasgow stages a scene echoing Hardy's *Tess of the d'Urbervilles*, a tale of female betrayal avenged that was itself a reaction against prevailing representations of women in fiction.[13] After fleeing the place where she first espied Jason and Geneva together, she decides to pay him a visit, believing that talking to him might somehow set things to rights. But, while staking out his home, she notices a shotgun, picks it up, and semiconsciously fires it in Jason's direction. Despite her intentions ("I tried to do it. I wanted to do it" [167]), Dorinda misses her target. On the one hand, this registers Glasgow's sense of life's arbitrariness—its lack of design—which Dorinda herself comes to apprehend later on. But, on the other, it signals Glasgow's recognition that having a heroine wither away under the strain of betrayal and having her executed for exacting mortal revenge (à la Hardy) are essentially one and the same: In both cases, woman places her fate entirely in the hands of love.[14]

By permitting Dorinda to pursue a path beyond the limited ones afforded to women in nineteenth-century fiction—even its most daring—the novel situates the protagonist's formation outside of the traditional plot of socialization. However, although we learn that "the ever-present sense of sin, which made the female mind in mid-Victorian literature resemble a page of the more depressing theology, was entirely absent from her reflections," we get no indication that a new way of thinking has replaced it (202). To put the point differently, even though her disenchantment with love inspires a new, renunciant mantra—"I've finished with all that"—it still leaves the old, exploratory one in place. That nagging question "What is Life?" persists and seems all the more urgent now that the old answers, love and marriage, have been ruled out.

Pine: The "Woman Adrift" Plot

In search of new answers, Dorinda absconds to New York. There a cab accident causes her to miscarry her illegitimate child. Thanks to the generosity of the surgeon who saves her life, she is able to start afresh. Moved by her sad case, the surgeon and his wife offer Dorinda lodging and comfortable employment—first, in Dr. Faraday's office and, eventually, in the Faraday household. As long as she remains in New York, where a macabre sort of serendipity frees her from the demands of adulthood, she can avoid her perfidious former lover and postpone coping with the pain of his betrayal. Miles away from Old Farm, she is able to skirt sacrifice and her responsibilities to her family and their virtually barren farm by periodically mailing contributions of sums that she is too well provided for to miss.

Pines—the plant that names this part of the novel—are, unlike broomsedge, solitary and strong, their movement ever upward and only marginally outward. No weeds leeching off the vitality of other plants, pines make their own ways in the world, soaring above their roots. These are the lineaments of the character type depicted in this next phase of *Barren Ground*'s exploration. Here Glasgow experiments with a more modern plotline for Dorinda, that of the "woman adrift." Taken up in some form by nearly all of Glasgow's contemporaries between 1900 and 1920, the "woman adrift" plotline was a staple of early-twentieth-century American fiction and had become the most popular mode of portraying single white women in the era's literature. Conceived in opposition to nineteenth-century sentimental fiction and courtship novels, the "woman adrift" novel narrates the life of a young white woman who leaves her rural home in search of a fuller life and grander prospects in the city. Unlike her nineteenth-century predecessors, this heroine is indifferent toward love and views men and marriage merely as means for acquiring wealth and status.

Even Glasgow succumbed to the "woman adrift" craze early in her career. Her scarcely remembered second novel, *Phases of an Inferior Planet* (1898), was in the vanguard of the trend, predating Dreiser's *Sister Carrie* and Grant's *Unleavened Bread* by two years. Its heroine and coprotagonist, Mariana—one of the period's earliest female social selves—quits her family's farm to pursue a career on the stage in New York. She marries but finds that wedlock in no way quiets her desire for self-display and recognition. Meanwhile, her husband, a ponderous scholar only slightly less bloodless than George Eliot's Casaubon, is run ragged and perpetually derailed from his "great work" in trying to satisfy her endless wants. Yet, eventually, he must confront a lesson that husbands in nineteenth-century fiction are usually spared: that "even a woman in love is not a woman always in love" (161). Once her infant dies (yet another macabre serendipity), Mariana's ties to domestic obligations are loosened just enough for her to justify leaving him to join a traveling opera company.

The contemporary reception of *Phases of an Inferior Planet* was mixed. Virtually every reviewer found the title perplexing, and, while agreeing that the novel showed promise, most thought it decidedly inferior to her debut novel, *The Descendant* (1897). One of the most recurrent objections to the novel, I believe, helps explain why Glasgow turned away from the urban "woman adrift" plotline in *Barren Ground*. That objection has to do with her treatment of human nature in *Phases*, which strained the credulity of many readers.[15] Though she does not reference *Phases* or the criticism it received, Glasgow attributes her return to the South, her homeland, to a wish to confront human nature, the very thing found wanting in her second novel. "My comprehension of Virginian life and manners," she writes, "was a knowledge of the blood, as well as the brain, and instinct warned me that here alone could I break through the surface of appearances and strike some vein of fundamental humanity" (*A Certain Measure* 153).

Glasgow's decision to situate many of her early novels in New York is understandable, given the stigma that the literary establishment of the time attached to fiction set outside of urban locations, works it frequently diminished with the designation "regionalist" or "local color." In the autumn of her long career, however, this expedient came to seem false to Glasgow. Dorinda experiences urges strikingly similar to Glasgow's, except that her return to the South is quite literal. Like Glasgow, she finds that she can begin to confront "real life" (one of the novel's most repeated phrases) only through confronting her roots and the culture most familiar to her. From the start, Dorinda's departure from Pedlar's Mill is depicted as more a flight from maturity than a step toward it. The journey to the city that had furnished so many male protagonists with the independence necessary to their maturation proves arresting for Dorinda. From the fantastical string of coincidences that ultimately frees her from motherhood—the car accident, the unlikely proximity of a "celebrated" surgeon to the scene of the accident, her full recovery with a convenient miscarriage to boot—to the boundless generosity of the family who employs her, everything about life in the city seems unreal. What Glasgow portrays as the least realistic aspect of all, however, is the supposition that escaping the familiar would bring Dorinda or the novel any closer to real life or maturity. In reflecting on the two years she has spent in New York, she perceives that "her outward existence had been altered by [her years spent away], but to her deeper self they had been scarcely more than dust blowing across her face" (231). Whiled away mostly under "the effects of an anæsthetic" (228), these years have contributed nothing to her maturation.

It is music that awakens her from this anaesthetized state and points her toward the right path. As the notes of Bach and Chopin permeate the concert hall, "pure sensation held and tortured her," forcing her "deep below the depths of her being" (239). This unmediated sensation stirs overwhelming feelings that the distractions of the city had enabled her to suppress. They provide the jolt she needs in order to feel the pull of "deeper associations . . . reaching out to her," associations "drawing her back across time and space and forgetfulness" (244). Her ears now attuned to the importunities of adulthood, she confesses to herself, "I feel as if the farm were calling to me to come back and help it" (244).

Life Ever-Lasting: Glasgow's Communitarian Alternative

Although at least one reader has criticized *Barren Ground* for its "individualistic" philosophy, the breaking of familiar ties in the novel comes to seem less a bold statement of autonomy than puerile egotism.[16] Growth, according to the novel, obliges one to embrace relatedness. And this concept is emblematized by the flower that names this final section. Everlastings are shrubs whose resplendent flowers sprout in bunches and spread outward, seemingly intent on sharing their beauty as widely as possible and on enmeshing themselves within their environs. Here we find subjective development rooted in social relations, what Jane Flax would call a "feminist deconstruction of the self" (232). But we'd err to assume, based on this, that the novel recircumscribes female subjectivity within the affectively charged space of domesticity. To do so would be to reaffirm the nineteenth century's "separate spheres" ideology as well as its division of society into nuclear familial units—terms that the novel has already rejected in its repudiation of the nineteenth-century marriage plot (or seduction narrative, which is, ideologically, the same thing). Having at once insisted that affiliation is the key to maturation and yet renounced the prevailing mode for affiliating (i.e., marriage and domesticity), the novel is faced with the challenge of generating a new affiliative paradigm for its heroine.

And this is where *Barren Ground* is its most inventive. To clear space for its new paradigm, after Dorinda returns to Old Farm from New York, the novel drives her blood relatives out of the home, one by one. First, her father dies of a stroke; later, Rufus, her younger brother, is forced to flee Pedlar's Mill after murdering a man; finally, the pious Mrs. Oakley, enervated by a life of ceaseless drudgery, expires under the psychological strain of being forced to perjure herself to protect Rufus from the law. But, significantly, these unfortunate events do not leave Dorinda in isolation; they provide her the opportunity to enrich her understanding of what it means to be related.

Though Dorinda does eventually marry, the eccentricities of her marriage demonstrate her adoption of a radical new outlook on affiliation. Initially, she refuses Nathan Pedlar's proposal, telling herself, as she had when proposed to in New York, that she is "finished with all that." She consents only after she sees the practical benefits of the union—its advantages for her farm—and he assures her that he "wouldn't want to interfere with [her]" (by which we are meant to infer, in part, that he will impose no sexual demands) (365). Far from an end in itself, her marriage serves as the means for her to reestablish a sense of community in Pedlar's Mill, the means to suture a populace sundered by its individualistic inward turns. Her extraordinarily practical marriage to Nathan Pedlar, for instance, has a rather corporate feel: Portrayed less as the establishment of an intimate nuclear family than as the creation of a partnership between equals, it is an arrangement in which the proprietary boundaries separating Oakley interests from Pedlar collapse. Through marriage, as Dorinda notes, his problems (raising the children his wife's death had left entirely to his care) become hers, and hers (developing the farm) become his. On its own, this example might seem to evince not the erosion of domestic outlines but simply their widening; indeed, it might strike one that this union provides the occasion for Nathan to expand his paternal authority.

Yet this is not how the novel portrays it. For one, as his promise that she "might have things [her] own way" suggests, theirs is a markedly nonhierarchical space, completely lacking the paterfamilias conferring identity upon and thus individuating the bourgeois home (365). Their partnership gives them the opportunity to revitalize barren ground and extend their improvement efforts to the larger space around them. The novel archly underscores Nathan's status as instrument by killing him off when he has outlived his use—once Dorinda has become the legal guardian of his children and he has taught her as much about farming as he could. Even the details of his death are telling. He is killed in a train wreck, but only because, after having escaped the wreckage safely, he returns to rescue screaming women, playing chivalrous knight to damsels in distress. In so disposing of Nathan, the novel smothers male protectiveness in its own smoke and rids Dorinda of yet another appurtenance of traditional domesticity.[17]

It becomes increasingly clear that Dorinda's skills and talents belong to the community, not to her husband or home. It is she who initiates all the efforts to improve living conditions in Pedlar's Mill, including the renovation of the roads. In contrast to the capitalistic configuration of the Ellgoods' Green Acres, in which wealth turns inward, Dorinda's prosperity translates into communal prosperity. The distinction between the Ellgoods and Dorinda is exemplified by their differing responses to Jason Greylock's misfortunes—his alcoholism and consequent transfer to the local poorhouse. Once Geneva Greylock (née Ellgood) dies, in James Ellgood's view, Jason's ties to the Ellgood family are severed and, with them, his claim to the family's support. From an individualistic perspective, the Ellgoods are blameless, even if not noble, in their neglect: Technically, they owe this nonrelative nothing, and any succor they choose to offer him would be charity, not duty. But Dorinda's ethics are much too communitarian for such laissez-faire thinking, though she has more cause than anyone else to savor his demise. Although she "had longed to punish him for his treachery," she feels compelled to take him in and nurse him during his final days (483). She is able to see him simply as a fellow inhabitant of Pedlar's Mill desperately in need of her help, her resentment yielding to the urgency of his situation.

Not only is Dorinda's embrace of relatedness strong enough to overcome past injustices committed against her; it is too great even for the divisive distinction of race. This claim may surprise some, in light of the numerous charges of racism that have been leveled against Glasgow.[18] It's undeniable that Glasgow is often obtuse in her handling of race, not least in her reliance on tired stereotypes in sketching her black characters. However, it seems unfair that these embarrassments—grievous though they surely are—should eclipse the salutary implications for Southern race relations inhering in *Barren Ground*'s communitarian vision. In characterizing Dorinda's relationship with her black domestic helper, Fluvanna, the narrator observes, "The affection between the two women had outgrown the slender tie of mistress and maid, and had become as strong and elastic as the bond that holds relatives together" (349). An affection as strong and elastic as the bond that holds relatives together: In using the intimacy of kinship as a figure for the relationship between these women, the novel at once underscores the intensity of that relationship and dethrones consanguinity from its status as primary mediator of human affiliation.

Similarly, when a flu outbreak afflicts her black neighbors, Dorinda rushes to their aid and, in the process, forges a bond with a part of the community whom a long history of exploitation had estranged. The novel anticipates the temptation to dismiss Dorinda's radical communitarianism as just another instance of benevolent white womanhood by demonstrating the reciprocity of her relations with her black neighbors. Her indiscriminate charitableness— "nonpersonal giving," in Linda Wagner's words (78)—is richly repaid. For instance, when war deprives Pedlar's Mill of the majority of its white male labor, Dorinda alone is able to secure hands among the local black youth while her white neighbors' crops, including the Ellgoods', run to ruin. The strength of Dorinda's bonds with her black neighbors gives rise to the kind of reciprocity that recognition of ineluctable relatedness inspires: Conscious of the interconnectedness of their lives, they regard securing one another's well-being as indistinguishable from securing their own. The aim here is not to acquit Dorinda or Glasgow of any and all charges of racism; it is, rather, to demonstrate Dorinda's oneness with the community to which she was born.

It is in this oneness with the community that Dorinda discovers real life and maturity. This rooted sense of self compels her to place the good of the community ahead of her own interests—or, more precisely, to regard these two considerations as identical. This view of the self entails the acknowledgment of both predetermined relations (relations based on circumstances of birth, shared histories, communal ties) and the involuntary obligations following from these relations. In so doing, it dispenses with the premium that liberal individualism places on consent and self-determination and its insistence, in some formulations, on the priority of the individual to society. It is a conviction that almost certainly would have been too risky for the nineteenth-century European novel, given its anti-aristocratic agenda.

Though the pragmatists shared Glasgow's awareness that selfhood in the United States of their time had to be reconceived in more associational terms, none theorized the communitarian subject that takes shape in *Barren Ground*. Such a conception of the self would not appear in philosophy for another sixty-odd years, in a more recent confrontation with liberal individualism. Because this theory so lucidly captures the vision at the heart of Glasgow's novel, it merits detailed elaboration here.

In his 1981 *After Virtue*, Alasdair MacIntyre proposes the notion of "narrative selfhood."[19] As fellow political philosopher Michael Sandel explains, MacIntyre, like Sandel himself, belongs to the group of 1980s philosophers who attempted to upend the individualistic, liberal and libertarian theories sprouting in the 1970s (chiefly, in the respective works of John Rawls and Robert Nozick) (249). Unlike the blank slates presupposed in such theories, MacIntyre suggests that a great deal of our identity precedes us—that we all inherit "a variety of debts, inheritances, rightful expectations and obligations" simply by virtue of the associations with which we are born as daughters and sons of someone, citizens of someplace, members of some socioeconomic class, and so forth (220). The stories of our lives, he claims, are "always embedded in the story of those communities" from which we derive our identities and have much less to do with the individual choices we make in our own lives than Lockean versions of liberalism maintain (221).

This version of rooted selfhood differs significantly from that often associated with the classical Bildungsroman. As Moretti argues, that narrative *ends* with the character's achievement of "organic totality" and "socialization" (57), and in it the decision to integrate must be one's own if it is to "become *legitimate*" (67). Glasgow's protagonist departs from this view in that she takes, as MacIntyre does, relatedness as the *given* of her life, not its product. For her, recognition of relation is where real life begins, not where it ends. One's life, Glasgow and MacIntyre suggest, is not entirely of one's own making—the product of personal choices—but, rather, dependent upon associations past and present.

In light of the realist novel's historical complicity with bourgeois political aspirations, as mentioned above, it is understandable that a view of selfhood along the lines of what MacIntyre suggests would not have predominated in nineteenth-century fiction. But it is important to note that, in his view, an acknowledgment of inherited relations in no way restricts individual potential, as Dorinda's story demonstrates. To quote MacIntyre once more, acknowledging such relations "does not entail that the self has to accept the moral *limitations* of the particularity of those forms of community. Without those moral particularities to begin from there would never be anywhere to begin; but it is in moving forward from such particularity that the search for the good, for the universal, consists" (221).

Born within a social stratum "midway between the lower gentility and the upper class of 'poor white'" yet ending life as one of the most prominent farmers in the state of Virginia and a pillar of her community, Dorinda shows that one needn't deny the claims of predetermined relations in order to advance. She needn't break from the community of Pedlar's Mill (by, say, starting from scratch in New York) in order to pursue the good. In fact, the novel suggests, breaking from these connections, extracting herself from the world in which her own life story is inseparably intertwined, would be as stunting to her as deracination to a flower: In New York, "earlier and deeper associations, *rooted there in the earth*, were reaching out to her . . ." (244; my emphasis).

And something similar is true of the novel that contains her. It does not ignore the body of literary conventions that precedes it; it takes this inheritance as its starting point, modifying these conventions to articulate its unique vision. By dramatizing its maturation as a progression through the patterns passed down to it, the novel treats the legacy of Anglo-American fiction not as an unwilled tie it has to cut but as a rich birthright from which it departs and without which it could not exist. Glasgow takes Wharton's axiom, "Convention is the first necessity of all art," a step farther. Together, each in their own ways, both Dorinda and the novel suggest that convention, a kind of inheritance, is the first necessity not only of art but of life as well.

Barren Ground's self-reflective approach seems quite timely when we consider how the literary landscape was changing in the 1920s, the decade in which her novel appeared in print. The modernists, the generation of writers just following Glasgow and her contemporaries, were reshaping fiction in the United States around the time of *Barren Ground*'s publication, with Fitzgerald's paradigmatic *Gatsby* appearing in the same year as Glasgow's novel. The so-called Lost Generation, we know, was extremely hostile to its Victorian past and made experimentation the rule in literary production. In the confrontations that *Barren Ground* stages between past literary modes and modern conditions, it offers an alternative model for artistic innovation that avoids the aggression toward the past characteristic of modernism. In this revisionary model—in which new modes of representation are narratively shown to emerge from the obsolescence of older ones—the past is treated not as the enemy of the present but as the necessary condition of its existence. At the same time, Glasgow's receptive attitude toward history—which allows for revision through the "annulment *and* the preservation of the past"[20]—reminds us of the breadth and variability of both literary realism and specifically the Bildungsroman. For *Barren Ground* teaches us that, though these literary forms emerged in tandem with liberal individualism, they could be combined with other conceptions of subjectivity to formulate original visions of the social world.

CHAPTER FOUR

Created in Her Image

Remaking the Business Tycoon in American Fiction

The only lasting epiphany in the vertiginous life of Undine Spragg, protagonist of Edith Wharton's *The Custom of the Country* (discussed at length in chapter 2), occasions what is probably that novel's most memorable line. In describing Undine's revelation that she had been hunting small game before shifting her ambitions from her American countrymen to the European aristocracy, the novel slips into free-indirect discourse, permitting the narrator's voice and Undine's mind to declare as one, "Every Wall Street term had its equivalent in the language of Fifth Avenue" (329). This formulation is remarkable for a number of reasons. For one, it is among the rare instances when Wharton's ironic narrator does not distance herself from Undine, an unusual moment in which author and protagonist might be understood as agreeing. Moreover, it eschews hierarchy and positions its two spheres—business and fashion, production and consumption, man's province and woman's—on a level plane. And, finally, Wharton's formulation is tantalizingly silent on the question of sequence, of priority. We are left wondering—adapting the question for our purposes—whether the Elmer Moffatt type (charismatic male business mogul) preceded the Undine Spragg type (charming female social climber) or vice versa. While the prevailing account of late-nineteenth- and early-twentieth-century

American history yields one answer for how this played out—positing the transition from an economy of scarcity to one of abundance as prerequisite for a culture of consumption—literary history, as we shall see, intimates a more nuanced alternative.

With remarkable efficiency, Wharton's novel offers a compelling outline of this alternative history, whose lineaments are sketched by her cocktail-party savant, Charles Bowen. Indemnifying Undine for her selfishness and grasping ways, Bowen describes the young woman as a "monstrously perfect result of the system," a mercenary system that has shifted "the emotional center of gravity" from the "drawing-room" to "the office" (127). At first glance, Bowen's observation would appear an affirmation of the prevailing historiography, even if it expresses that historiography in terms less economic than intimate: The businessman precedes modern America's insatiable woman, the latter the resentful product of the former's single-minded focus on his affairs. In this, Bowen accords with *The Nation*'s reviewer quoted in chapter 1, who asseverated that "we are undoubtedly in the position of having placed woman on a pedestal and left her there lonely and rather dizzy" (rev. of *Custom* 494).

But this is only half the story. Wharton makes it clear in the novel that Bowen, like many in her old-moneyed set, are blinded by prejudice, nostalgic rather than realistic. The insipid slaves to business whom both Bowen and *The Nation*'s reviewer envision have become, by the second decade of the twentieth century, relics of an earlier generation—and, as we shall see, are being replaced by a new vision of the business tycoon. The type that Bowen disparages belongs to the first generation of American realist writers. To grasp as much, we need look no farther than the business novels of that generation's preeminent practitioners, Henry James and William Dean Howells. The avaricious protagonists of James's *The American* (1877) and of Howells's *The Rise of Silas Lapham* (1885) are, without question, two of the flattest main characters ever created by these novelists. For writers renowned precisely for a penchant for deep characterization, a deviation of this kind cannot help but seem deliberate, and I understand it as an indication of their view of the hollowness of the businessman of their time. To register this hollowness, James makes his Christopher Newman (whose very name marks him as a parvenu) a millionaire "collector," which, we quickly learn, indexes a fetishistic drive for acquisition without the capacity to appreciate the fruits of that drive. Howells, in turn, presents us with a character whose own wife "perceived that his paint was something more than business to him" (44). Continuing the burlesque of Lapham's interior life, the narrator tells us that the paint business "was a sentiment, almost a passion" (44). In another novel, *A Modern Instance* (1882), Howells gives us the closest thing to a social self he has ever offered in his protagonist, the enterprising journalist Bartley Hubbard, who is cast in opposition to the nobler Ben Halleck, a man said to possess "character" (361). Bartley, by contrast, is described by Halleck as "a poor, cheap sort of creature. Deplorably smart and regrettably handsome" (213). Marking Bartley's social adaptability, Halleck calls him a "fellow that assimilated everything to a certain extent, and nothing thoroughly. A fellow with no more nature than a base-ball" (213). Bartley—and the modern forces he represents—is sensationally ejected from the novel, leaving the more anchored, old-fashioned selves to contemplate the moral dilemma of divorce and remarriage and the limits of personal freedom (good liberal individuals that they are). The nineteenth-century businessman, depicted as the antithesis of culture, is scarcely a welcome guest in "the house of fiction" (to invoke James's famous phrase), his presence therein more often a means of renouncing values considered incompatible with literature and the arts generally.

In her first major novel, Wharton herself succumbed to the view of the businessman as the antithesis of culture. *The House of Mirth* (1905) is an elegy for beauty in an era dominated by commerce and consumption. As countless critics have pointed out, Lily Bart's very name (not to mention the novel's title, borrowed from the New Testament) links her with a figure associated with transcendent beauty—"the lilies of the field," referenced in Christ's "Sermon on the Mount," that "toil not, neither do they spin" (Matt. 6:28).[1] Lily is beauty incarnate, beauty for its own sake, but she finds her quest to soar above the crass world of New York's high society stymied both by that society's propensity toward exploitation and by the importunate money problem bound to bedevil any young lady with champagne tastes but a Budweiser budget. We find Wharton vividly maintaining the divide between the aesthetic realm and the commercial in the sharp contrast she creates between Lily's suitors:

The ethereal and ostentatiously artistic "republic of the spirt" of Lawrence Selden is pitted against the cold-blooded mercenary calculation of Simon Rosedale. The promise of a life filled with art and culture and free of the encumbrances of need and work that Selden uses to tantalize Lily proves nonviable in the Gilded Age, and Wharton underscores this fact by exposing the spokesperson for such a vision as a sham: More content to contemplate Lily as an aesthetic and philosophical question than inclined to help her in her hour of desperation, Selden disappoints capitally. Rosedale, by contrast, offers her a way out of her predicament that involves blackmailing her rival. However, clinging to aristocratic values utterly out of keeping with her moment—her fruitless "nobility," as Wai Chee Dimock describes it ("Debasing Exchange" 789)—Lily rejects the Rosedale option and, in effect, seals her own fate. Hers is a problem of adaptability, an incapacity to reconcile her aesthetic sensibility with the new world order ushered in by American modernization.

Might this obduracy have taken root in Lily's creator as well? After all, as much as Wharton writes off Selden as bogus, we have no indication that she finds much appealing in Rosedale, no matter that his hard-nosed practicality almost certainly would have saved Lily. However, her rank aversion to what Rosedale represents (tinged as it is with antisemitism) would not endure throughout her career. If, as Elaine Showalter argues in "The Death of the Lady (Novelist)," *The House of Mirth* was Wharton's way of killing her inner lady so that she could write serious fiction, it also constitutes a step away from the rearguard, anti-business prejudices that made *The House of Mirth* less an exploration of a new world than a lament for a world bygone—prejudices that it would take thirty years for her equally aristocratic older friend, Henry James, to recognize.[2] It took Wharton far less time than James to begin removing her reactionary blinders, for, by the time she wrote *The Custom of the Country* less than a decade later, she was not so intent on averting her gaze from the literary potential of business.

In that novel, even such a sophisticate as Ralph Marvell is able to exclaim of Elmer Moffatt, without irony, "Jove, I wish I could put him in a book!" (154) and, even more provocatively, later wonder why the penetrating insight shown by the businessman "did not qualify every financier to be a novelist" (159). How did we get, over the

course of only a single generation, from one vision of the businessman to another so radically its opposite? How is it that, for James
and Howells, the businessman was the novel's object of ridicule
while, for Wharton and her contemporaries, he would become a
viable novelistic subject, elevated at times to a status near-heroic?
Certainly, the economic shift from manufacture to finance in the
United States entailed a corresponding shift in the skillset required
of the man of affairs: Now deals and relationships, not industriousness, were what drove success in the marketplace. But something
different was necessary to make this new figure, so wholly unlike
his forebear, legible in the cultural imagination.

The answer to this problem, it turns out, is Undine, whose role in
this literary transformation is overdetermined. On the one hand, it
is Moffatt's desire to win back Undine that propels him to such prodigious successes. For example, when he sees her in the sumptuous
estate in Faubourg during her marriage to the French count, Moffatt
gamely observes, "You always *were* a lap ahead of me," suggesting
his efforts to keep up (327). On the other hand, that Undine is prerequisite to the invention of the mogul Elmer Moffatt is emblematic
of the transformation of the businessman in American fiction more
broadly. What I am proposing is that the project of reimagining
American women in fiction—a project traced in the preceding chapters of this study—proved positively indispensable in the slightly
later effort to reimagine the American business tycoon.

Why did this figure need to be reimagined in the first place?
There are several reasons. One has been adumbrated already: In
earlier fiction, such as that of Howells and James, he had functioned
as the repository for everything that the patrician class despised
about the industrializing nation—its rapacity, rootlessness, and
lack of culture. This attitude even antedates the first generation of
literary realism, evident in such antebellum works as Herman Melville's "Bartleby, the Scrivener: A Story of Wall-Street" (1853) and,
more obliquely, Edgar Allan Poe's "The Purloined Letter" (1844).[3]
In a word, the first generation of realist writers simply could not
accurately depict business culture or the business tycoon for the
fact that these writers—consumed by resentment over what Alan
Trachtenberg calls "the incorporation of America"—were in no
position to look at the world of commerce dispassionately. James,

as I intimate above, would admit as much himself when reflecting on what he characterized as his "romantic," wish-fulfilling bent in writing *The American*. Both born considerably before the moment in American history that would produce the wide-scale socioeconomic changes cementing the ascendancy of big business, Howells and James were far more susceptible to reactionary positions than the next generation, who came of age when this cultural transformation was more or less a fait accompli.

Another reason why the early-twentieth century demanded a revision of the business tycoon is the changing face of the ruling class in this country—a merger, as Nancy Glazener has shown, of the first families with a rising class of wealthy professionals. This shift, Glazener demonstrates, had implications for various cultural institutions, from museums to magazines. At a moment when novelists—who, like all artists, once defined themselves in opposition to market values—were professionalizing, and when the leading artistic institutions depended on the patronage of newly minted business moguls, how ever could writers maintain the nineteenth century's view of commerce and art as constituting separate spheres? This was an era when the business tycoon's dominance was not only economic but also cultural; like it or not, all had to acknowledge that business was at the center of American culture. Therefore, as self-professed realist writers and recorders of the American scene, this generation of novelists could not in good conscience allow whatever antipathy they felt for business to prevent them from exploring its literary potential, no matter that this antipathy remained firmly in place. In other words, although they might hold anti-business sentiments, these writers refused to ignore the historical change staring them in the face.

DREISER'S *THE FINANCIER*

As suggestive as Wharton's career is in thinking about the connection between reimagining women in fiction and reimagining the business tycoon, it is in Theodore Dreiser's work that this connection is most apparent. Unlike Wharton, who eventually reached the point where she could portray business culture seriously in the background of what are essentially novels of manners, Dreiser wrote *business* novels. In tackling the phenomenon head-on, he produced some of his era's most absorbing dramas of American business and most striking depictions of the business tycoon, and only twelve years after *Sister Carrie* was published. In 1912, Dreiser published the first installment of what would become his *Trilogy of Desire*, a saga inspired by the sensational life of Chicago magnate Charles Tyson Yerkes Jr., infamous for his nefarious conquest of the city's street railways. "But," as Philip Gerber rightly observes, "to think of *Trilogy of Desire* merely as a biography manqué or as a roman à clef is to approach it in the most superficial terms" (xi).

Gerber notes several of the liberties that Dreiser takes with Yerkes's history, but the most telling of Dreiser's artistic licenses is one that Gerber does not note, the novel's anachronism.[4] Dreiser's Yerkes-inspired protagonist, Frank Cowperwood, is, of course, not Dreiser's contemporary. Old enough to have served in the Union Army, Cowperwood is the same age as Howells's and James's fictional businessmen, both of whom, unlike Cowperwood, served. (For Cowperwood, "the freedom of the negro was not a significant point" [85].) And yet, time and again, we find the narrator employing a discourse that would not be in vogue until the twentieth century, Dreiser's time. For example, Cowperwood's father, we are told, "believed sincerely that vast fortunes were to be made out of railroads if one only had the capital and that curious thing, a magnetic personality—the ability to win the confidence of others," but that he lacked "magnetism and vision" and was therefore destined for mediocrity (2). By contrast, his son, our protagonist, is repeatedly described as "magnetic," his successes almost uniformly attributed in some measure to his charisma. Such language, we recall from chapter 2, belongs squarely to what Warren Susman characterizes as the age of "personality," the modality that supplanted "character" when the nation exchanged an economy centered on production for one centered on consumption. It is rather unlikely, then, that a man born in the 1830s, much less his father, would set much store by personality. The point is not to expose Dreiser for presentism, for he was well aware of what he was doing.[5] I wish simply to demonstrate the lengths to which this novelist went to rehabilitate the business tycoon for his era. This rehabilitation project compelled Dreiser to reinterpret the magnate and his triumphs according to the terms of success recognizable to an early-twentieth-century audience.

But there's more still to this anachronistic move. Had Dreiser wished simply to give the business tycoon a makeover, he easily could have set the story in his own time, just as he had in writing *Sister Carrie*, whose protagonist fits entirely within her historical moment (as the many other woman-centered novels of the time suggest). So why time-travel so far into the past? Dreiser offered this explanation for his story's setting: The period "featured singular examples of 'mental action spurred by desire, ambition, vanity, without any of the moderating influence which we are prone to admire—sympathy, tenderness and fair play'" (qtd. in Zimmerman 194). And yet Dreiser's own moment—whose rapacity Howells and others tirelessly denounced and which saw, only a few years earlier, the publication of Sinclair's *The Jungle*—could not, from any anamorphic angle, be viewed as possessing any such "moderating influence," certainly not "sympathy, tenderness, and fair play."

However, aside from this spurious rendering of his own historical moment as vastly more humane in commerce than the previous epoch, there are other, more plausible reasons why this antebellum setting might have appealed to Dreiser. On the one hand, it made Cowperwood the contemporary of Howells's and James's fictional businessmen. Although each novel captures its protagonist at a different stage of life—Dreiser's is in his youth, James's approaching middle age, and Howells's in senescent decline—all three characters were born in the 1830s, the Jacksonian age of rugged individualism. In creating a conflicting account of the mid-nineteenth-century businessman, Dreiser agonistically puts his version into competition with those of his predecessors. If he had set the story in the late-nineteenth or early-twentieth century, there would be no conflict; we might conclude simply that the businessman just underwent a transformation over time, as most things do. However, Dreiser is not suggesting that this figure has undergone a change since the earlier days of his literary forerunners; he is suggesting that his forerunners were wrong about him.

On the other hand, setting the story so far into the past helps Dreiser skirt the risk of feminizing the business tycoon. As I have shown in the foregoing chapters, the second generation of American realist writers first used women to conceive of selfhood outside the individualist terms of the nineteenth-century realist novel. Positioning the magnetic, mutable Cowperwood historically prior to Carrie and her sisters makes them seem derivative rather than the other way around, as was actually the case. It places men at the helm of cultural change and creates the impression of a cultural trickle-down in which men simply hand down from the top a new cultural dispensation to a quiescent generation of women. This is historical legerdemain on Dreiser's part, for it was writing Carrie that enabled Dreiser to write Cowperwood; it was thinking through cultural change via women that enabled Dreiser to think in new terms about the lives of men. Dreiser's historical ruse seems to have worked well, given that, while at least one scholar has noted the Carrie-like attributes of Cowperwood, no one has attributed their provenances to Carrie. For example, in his authoritative overview of American business fiction, David Zimmerman notes, "Dreiser delineates an inescapably intersubjective conception of individuality, one that comprehends the superman only in relation to the social, economic, and historical arenas in which he gains his power and acts out his desire. What sets Dreiser apart from earlier business fiction writers, except perhaps Norris, is that he refuses to be alarmed or scandalized by this dissolution of personal sovereignty" (421–22). While Zimmerman perceptively describes the nonindividualist aspects of Dreiser's businessman—"intersubjective," bereft of "personal sovereignty"—he fails to link them to the first, most famous, and most manifestly nonindividualist protagonist Dreiser ever wrote, Carrie Meeber. In fact, he emphasizes their differences, wishing—erroneously, I contend—to read "*The Financier* as a tale of 'accounting' rather than as a tale of desire" (195).[6] (I'll recur to Zimmerman's observation later, but for different reasons.)

Before discussing the striking parallels between Dreiser's project of reimagining the tycoon and the wider project of reimagining women of which *Sister Carrie* is a crucial part, I want to identify an important feature of Cowperwood that we do not find in Carrie: his acute artistic bent. Although, during his schooldays, he thought literature "silly" and Latin "of no use"—preferring, predictably, "bookkeeping and arithmetic"—Cowperwood turns out to be quite the art connoisseur (13). "During the years in which he had been growing into manhood," explains the narrator, "he had come instinctively into manhood," explains the narrator, "he had come instinctively into sound notions of what was artistic and refined" (59). This is one of the most curious aspects of the novel—the way it interrupts its narrations of Cowperwood's complex business dealings with long, digressive tracts detailing his artistic discernment. This attribute is too conspicuous to be accidental, the awkward shifts from Cowperwood's ledgers to his "lovely collections of Japanese ivories" too jarring not to be significant.

On the one hand, it offers a way of endowing him with the same sharp social instincts that we observe in Carrie, to whom Dreiser ascribes "an innate taste for imitation and no small ability" (112). But why, in Cowperwood's case, make this point via art? Following Walter Benn Michaels's view of Dreiser as capitalist culture's novelist par excellence, we might understand Dreiser as enacting a full-scale repudiation of the nineteenth century's distinction between the realms of business and art, a distinction, as we have seen, that already had come to seem tenuous in Wharton's *The House of Mirth*, published seven years earlier.[7] As Dreiser sees it, no sphere falls outside business's purview, and, unlike many of his contemporaries in the arts, he is able to treat this idea dispassionately, as an accomplished fact rather than an abomination warranting endless handwringing. Art is a business: "'He [another young man intensely interested in painting] tells me great pictures are going to increase in value,'" reports Cowperwood to an art-importer acquaintance, "'and what I could get for a few hundred thousand now will be worth millions later'" (162). And business is an art: "Buying and selling stocks, as he had soon learned, was an art, a subtlety, almost a psychic emotion. Suspicion, intuition, feeling—these were the things to be 'long' on" (43).[8] Moreover, just as Dreiser transforms the realist novel from a venue inhospitable to the business tycoon into his rightful home, he shifts the businessman himself from an unlettered lout to a potential novelist: "A student of finance once observed that nothing is so sensitive as money, and the financial mind partakes largely of the quality of the thing in which it deals" (390).

The idea invoked in the previous sentence—of a mind partaking of the quality of the thing in which it deals—recalls the central argument of Michaels's well-known study of turn-of-the-century realism, *The Gold Standard and the Logic of Naturalism*. In associating the fictions of Dreiser and his contemporaries with capitalism, he finds in money, in greenbacks, a homology with characterization in these works. Drawing on the logic of "internal difference" that Marx has told us structures commodities, Michaels sees the fictive beings in these novels as propelled by "the logic of the gold standard, the desire to make [themselves] equal to [their] face value" (22). For him, it is the endurance of a sense of internal difference that sustains desire in these ever-striving characters, fitting them for a culture of consumption.

Dreiser's own first reference to gold in *The Financier*, however, hints at an alternative explanation for the insatiability of desire in Frank Cowperwood and, by extension, for the source of his characterization. In an early scene focusing on Cowperwood's adolescent days, we are told that he "was a financier by instinct, and all the knowledge that pertained to that great art was as natural to him as the emotions and subtleties of life are to a poet. This medium of exchange, *gold*, interested him intensely" (8). In addition to conjuring for the nth time Dreiser's conjunction of the businessman with the man of letters, this description of Cowperwood may appear fetishistic—an allusion, perhaps, to Trina Sieppe, the ill-fated female lead in Frank Norris's 1899 novel *McTeague* who onanistically caresses but never spends her hoard of gold coins. Had Dreiser written simply, "*Gold* interested him intensely," we would have persuasive grounds for viewing his protagonist as a butch Trina. But, in fact, the depiction of Cowperwood here brings him closer to Dreiser's own heroine of 1899, Carrie Meeber, than to Norris's. In linking the financier's interest in gold to its exchange function, Dreiser emphasizes the fundamentally social nature of Cowperwood's desire. As we have seen, Carrie values currency for social reasons as well, conceiving of it in distinctly other-directed terms: "Money: something everybody else has and I must get" (45).

I am suggesting that Dreiser figures the business tycoon as a social self, the same paradigm for selfhood on which he and his contemporaries drew so extensively in envisioning white women in the preceding decades. Shortly I will explain Cowperwood's social selfhood more fully, but I first want to reiterate how this mode of selfhood leads to the endless desire that Michaels—intriguingly but, I contend, mistakenly—attributes to a cultural logic predicated upon capitalistic internal difference. In fact, it is the instinctive pursuit of assimilation with the outside world, not differentiation within, that stokes desire in the social self. Recall that George Herbert Mead posits the social self as an almost-ceaselessly mutable being, her desires—all strivings, aspirations, preferences—dictated by a dynamic social world. Urban social landscapes, such as those that Cowperwood and his female counterparts inhabit, are dense and variegated and therefore consign social selves to paths of perpetual desiring and unending self-transformation.

Frank Cowperwood's much-mentioned "inscrutable eyes," oddly enough, offer an important clue into his social selfhood. At first glance, it would seem that such a feature would seal him off from the social world, enclose him within himself. On the one hand, this self-evident interpretation of his eyes is correct but not in a way that prevents us from viewing Cowperwood as a social self. Calling attention to the impenetrability or unknowability of a character is, as we have seen, one method in this era's fiction for suggesting that that character represents a new, ill-understood emergence in the cultural matrix. Chapter 1 leads with the example of Mrs. Sommers, the protagonist of Kate Chopin's short story "A Pair of Silk Stockings," a married woman who, in her newly-developed unorthodox disinclination toward domesticity and enchantment by desire, puzzles her probing male fellow passenger on the trolley. Similarly, Cowperwood's inscrutability could be construed as serving Dreiser's effort to proffer him as a new species.

On the other hand, that "you could tell nothing by [his eyes]" signals the subjective vacancy essential to the ever-wanting social self, the constitutional lack that guarantees the insatiability of desire. Cowperwood contains no established core of selfhood from which his desires and commitments spring; these latter invade him from the outside world insensibly, with little or no intercession on his part. This is why, in the portrayals of Cowperwood's strivings, drive is consistently far more emphasized than any object of desire. In Dreiser's depiction of Cowperwood's attraction to his soon-to-be wife, Lillian, for example, the drive impelling him toward the woman receives more attention than the beloved: "Something chemic and hence dynamic was uppermost in him now and clamoring for expression" (136). These two aspects of Cowperwood's oft-referenced inscrutability work hand in hand: The fact that there is nothing visible in him—no stable, identifiable core—is precisely what renders him unrecognizable to the unreconstructed subjects whom he so confounds. Unlike Cowperwood and the black grouper at the center of the bizarre conceit that ends the novel (in what is probably this fish's debut in serious fiction), these outdated observers of Cowperwood lack the "almost unbelievable power of simulation" (501) because they are too *selved*, their subjective essences and their identities too anchored. And so they remain hopelessly incapable of understanding a being who, by contrast, always understands them perfectly.

But let us return to Cowperwood's eyes, for, if the eyes are the windows to the soul, we might justifiably regard him as soulless, an insult not infrequently lobbed at financiers, in Dreiser's time as well as ours. It is important, though, to understand that Cowperwood's soullessness is no more malevolent than it is benevolent. When, for example, we encounter such disclosures in the novel as "His conscience was not troubled by that. He had none, truly," we are not meant to view Dreiser's financier as immoral since such a view would contravene the novel's attempt to present him as a social self, an unmoored subject ceaselessly in flux. Cowperwood is amoral, guided, as he says, by the Emersonian-sounding credo "I satisfy myself" (135). Ironically, this turns out to be less a statement of self-reliance than another permutation of Undine Spragg's extroverted formulation, "I want what others want" (*Custom* 61), for the satisfaction that he pursues is as variable as and is largely dictated by the social world and, ultimately, chimerical.

Cowperwood's lack of well-defined "noble theories of conduct" associates him not only with Undine but also with her business-mogul husband Elmer Moffatt, who, as Showalter aptly observes, possesses "a genuine disdain for religious piety and social cant" ("Spragg" 94). Perhaps more surprisingly, this trait also links him to the very definition of pragmatist philosophy put forth by the movement's leading practitioner. Pragmatism, according to William James, "has in fact no prejudices whatever, no obstructive dogmas, no rigid canons of what shall count as proof. She is completely genial. She will entertain any hypothesis, she will consider any evidence" (307). In the introduction, I expatiated on James's feminization of pragmatism, but what matters most here is the way he vacates pragmatism, a distinctly American philosophy, of all content. Partaking of pragmatism's seemingly inexhaustible malleability, Cowperwood's ethics, such as they are, prove as variable as the stock market.

It is just this moral flexibility that enables Cowperwood to abandon his first wife for a younger, more congenial one. To the prospective wife's father—Edward Butler, an upstanding pillar of the community wedded to the old ways—Cowperwood defends his dubious ambitions in the most dispassionate and pragmatic of terms: "In my judgment the present end justifies the means. The end I have in view is to marry Aileen" (382). Unsurprisingly, this justification does not in the least satisfy the severe patriarch, whose stubborn principles and anchored selfhood belong to a species entirely apart from Cowperwood's. And the irreconcilable differences between these two men spring from precisely the same source as those between Cowperwood and his first wife. Repeatedly described as "lymphatic," Lillian possesses none of Cowperwood's energy or drive. Significantly, she is his senior by five years, and this is her second marriage, her first husband having died. Here Dreiser makes use of a tactic that we have seen not only in his own novel *Sister Carrie* but also in those of his contemporaries—staging a battle between outdated and modern modes of selfhood through marrying the old-fashioned (and sometimes older) to the more dynamic (and sometimes younger). Only, this time, it is the reverse of the paradigm that we have been observing so far—what a chapter title of Jennifer Fleissner's *Women, Compulsion, Modernity* sums up as "The New Woman & the Old Man."

The irreconcilable differences between Cowperwood and Lillian require further elaboration, for they clarify Dreiser's conception of the business tycoon as harbinger of a new kind of American. We have seen already Cowperwood's flexible, pragmatic moral code. Lillian's is the opposite—a fact hinted at by the surname by which she is introduced to us, Semple, a thinly veiled allusion to her Victorian simplicity. More the product of the culture of character than that of personality, Lillian has all the convictions that a good nineteenth-century woman was expected to have; "she was a natural conservator of public morals" (136). Yet Dreiser wryly exposes the seams of this rigid morality, which, in Dreiser's day, were rapidly coming into view through the rise of psychoanalysis and sexology. For example, we get a glimpse of her priggish repressiveness when told that "she was ashamed of the passion that at times swept and dominated her" (136). Her fixity, like that of Edward Butler's, associates her with the old individualism, a model of selfhood in which one grows into what one is and remains that, settling into the static state that Franco Moretti terms "maturity."

Given Cowperwood's subjective constitution, it is little wonder that he should grow tired of his inert first wife—something husbands certainly did in nineteenth-century life but hardly ever in nineteenth-century fiction. As the narrator explains, "Sympathy and affection were great things"—things inextricably bound up with conceptions of nineteenth-century womanhood—"but desire and charm must endure or one was compelled to be sadly conscious of their loss" (79–80). The word *desire* is doing double duty here: The problem is not simply that desire for Lillian has waned in Cowperwood; it's also that his desire has waned because she has so suppressed her own. Not desiring enough, and therefore incapable of "mental alteration" (as the narrator elsewhere describes her), Lillian cannot possibly satisfy a man fetishistically obsessed with drive itself. The way the narrator describes Cowperwood's mounting discontent makes this clear: "He began to look at her at times with a speculative eye—not very critically, for he liked her—but with an attempt to weigh her personality. He had known her for five years and more now. What did he know about her? The vigor of youth—those first years—had made up for so many things, but now that he had her safely . . ." (65; ellipsis Dreiser's). Notably, the passage underscores that Cowperwood treats love no differently from the market and finance (a habit he shares with Wharton's Undine Spragg). But, more to the point, it also demonstrates how much in love he is with the chase and how much he fears the destination. Now having her—and a solid, unvarying *her*—he is left with nothing more to want, and that is tantamount to death in the tradition of realism that I have been tracing. (Recall the body count of desire-bereft men in chapter 2.)

In light of Cowperwood's insatiable desire, it is to be expected that nineteenth-century domesticity, with its orientation toward settling down, would be no less congenial to him than it is to the women characters of the previous chapters, from Chopin's discontented heroines onward. His is no simple Huck Finn–like aversion to "sivilization" but a constitutional incompatibility with Victorian selfhood—with what Gillian Brown memorably terms "domestic individualism."[9] Immediately after his awkwardly rendered courtship with Lillian, the narrator teases us with the possibility that Cowperwood's story might follow the trajectory of the conventional marriage plot, noting, "He was going to be very happy there now, he thought, with Lillian and possibly a brood of young Cowperwoods" (58). But already there are good reasons to doubt this forecast, not the least of which the fact that there are, at this point, hundreds of pages of the novel remaining (some 450 in my edition). Even fatherhood is shorn of all sentimentality and cast in an egotistical, avaricious light: "He liked it, the idea of self-duplication. It was almost acquisitive, this thought" (61). Interestingly, though, we find Dreiser seemingly expressing sympathy with his protagonist's unorthodox view of conjugality. Stepping away from narrating in order to solemnize, he writes, "It is a curious fact that by some subtlety of logic in the Christian world, it has come to be believed that there can be no love outside of the conventional process of courtship and marriage" (147).[10] In their conspicuous sympathy with the protagonist, such heavy-handed moments lend support to the view that Dreiser admired the amoral, capitalistic world that he so obsessively depicted, for they suggest that he admired the amoral capitalist.

Cowperwood's selection for Lillian's replacement reveals nearly as much as Dreiser's characterization of him. Unsurprisingly, part of Aileen's allure for Cowperwood consists in his love for the drive, his desire for all that he is told he cannot have—to wit, her father's strident objection to the match. But there is yet more that draws him to her. Dreiser leaves us in no doubt about the pair's compatibility, stating it outright: "They ran together temperamentally from the first like two leopards" (164). We suspect for a moment even that Dreiser is on the verge of switching gears and making the novel about her, hearing a narrative "On your mark!" in his disclosure, "She was eager for life. How was she to get it?" (89). But, of course, Dreiser already has pursued this plot in *Sister Carrie* and *Jennie*

Gerhardt, and the spotlight remains on the business tycoon, the emergent type he is intent on defining for his culture.

Still, Dreiser is careful to underscore that it is Aileen's social selfhood that makes her the perfect mate for the other-directed Cowperwood, referring to "her aggressive disposition, her love of attention, her vanity" (86) and rooting her desires firmly in the social ("She was chronically interested in men—what they would think of her—and how she compared with other women" [90]). Even if Dreiser's anachronistic portrayal of Cowperwood—his placement of a personality in the age of character—conveys the impression that the magnetic businessman preceded his feminine counterpart, the fact that Dreiser makes recourse to her to clarify the businessman's features signals his dependence on new conceptions of modern woman. We are reminded, no matter Dreiser's intentions, that he could not have imagined Cowperwood without first having imagined Carrie. At the same time, having Cowperwood abandon an old-fashioned woman is the narrative complement to his and his contemporaries' lopsided competition between the new woman and the old man: It signals these characters' modernity by showing who's not their type.

In view of Cowperwood's anchorless subjectivity, we understand the cleverly counterintuitive sense in which Dreiser casts the character's guiding mantra, "I satisfy myself." Without a stable self, there is no enduring satisfaction, only temporary landing pads on an unending journey toward more. In *Sister Carrie*, Dreiser, like his contemporaries, signals the insatiability of his protagonist's desire by dispensing with narrative closure and leaving Carrie still rocking with desire at the novel's conclusion. In *The Financier*, he dispenses with closure in a different way: Cowperwood's journey is extended over the span of two lengthy sequels, *The Titan* and *The Stoic*, which, with *The Financier*, constitute Dreiser's *Trilogy of Desire*. In what almost seems a token of the trilogy's unwillingness to end, Dreiser did not live to complete its last installment, *The Stoic*, published posthumously, the manuscript finished by the author's wife. It turns out that Dreiser was no less dependent on women for his literary representation than his fictional male characters were for theirs.

FRANK NORRIS: THE EXCEPTION THAT PROVES THE RULE

For one of Dreiser's eminent contemporaries, the matter was quite different. Although his name is routinely mentioned in the same breath as Dreiser's, Frank Norris's conception of the business tycoon could scarcely differ more. The chasm between these authors' visions of the businessman, I propose, is at least partially attributable to the chasm between their visions of modern woman. The second and final entry in Norris's own business trilogy manqué, *The Pit* (1903), begins with laser-like focus on its heroine, Laura Dearborn, but about halfway through makes a jarring detour toward the man who would become Laura's husband, business magnate Curtis Jadwin. Readers are primed by the novel's opening chapter—focusing on an orphaned ingenue dazzled by the big city—to expect yet another of the era's characteristic "What will she do next?" plots centering on modern young women, à la Dreiser's *Sister Carrie*, which appeared just three years prior. What a surprise, then, to witness the novel metamorphose abruptly into a *Rise of Silas Lapham* on steroids—surprise compounded by Norris's notorious contempt for Howells, expressed both in this novel and elsewhere.[11]

As Norris's decision to situate this plot pivot at the novel's midpoint suggests, the abruptness inflicted upon readers was almost certainly by design. Occurring right after Laura weds Jadwin, it serves to register the grating disharmony Norris discerned between domesticity and business. Such a view was hardly novel, of course, long preceding Howells's *Silas Lapham* and consonant with the nineteenth century's separate-spheres discourse, which posited women's sphere as the home (private) and men's as the wider world of affairs (public). What is new, however, is the antagonism between the two spheres. Midcentury Anglo-American culture imagined these two spheres as complementary, the home providing the moral and psychological depth required for a person (usually a man) to prosper in the world. By Howells's time, as we have seen, that cherished balance had been disrupted by the rapid ascendancy of commerce. This is one of the primary reasons for the pervasive fretting about the dissolution of the nuclear family (evinced by rising divorce rates and declining marriage rates) and about the vitiation of men's subjective lives (recall the caricature of Lapham).

As I have been suggesting, American novelists of the generation immediately following Howells and James's tended to depict the businessman not as insipid but as just the opposite—dynamic movers and shakers possessed of all the magnetism and energy widely attributed to modern women. Norris did not follow this tendency of his contemporaries. I will explain his deviations from the pattern in due course, but first it would be useful to consider briefly Norris's literary trajectory, since, as I'm claiming, there is a correlation, if not a causal link, between the way this generation of novelists wrote about modern women early in their careers and how they would envision the businessman later. Norris published *McTeague*, his most famous novel, only a year before Dreiser published *Sister Carrie*. Despite its title, this novel is almost as much about Trina Sieppe as it is about the ogrish dentist. Trina looks nothing like Dreiser's Carrie or, for that matter, like any of the other women characters we have been considering. Neither malleable nor especially charming, Trina differs from her fictional contemporaries most conspicuously in her circumscribed desire, circumscribed to the point of pathology. At first, there is little cause to be concerned about the McTeagues. In the initial phase of their married life, Trina—like a good middle-class wife—conducts her ménage with admirable economy, insisting that her lottery winnings be preserved as a nest egg and that the couple sustain themselves only on the modest combination of the interest from it and McTeague's earnings. As is frequently the case in Norris's fiction, however, the marriage begins to deteriorate as finances become strained—in this case, after McTeague loses his dental practice.

What comes to matter most, however, is that "McTeague had lost his ambition" and "all he wanted was a warm place to sleep and three good meals a day" (475). And what facilitates his sloth? The fact that Trina "supported their misfortunes with a silent fortitude" (476). McTeague becomes a mooch, the kind that one of Dreiser's heroines wouldn't have tolerated. As we saw in chapter 2, when Hurstwood reaches the point with Carrie where "all that he wanted of her was something to eat," she kicks him to the curb (274). That is one of the period's many novels repudiating nineteenth-century domesticity largely for the fact it is predicated on the notion that desire in women is satiable, dissipating upon marriage. By contrast, it views modern desire as dynamic and inexhaustible. This is not the case in *McTeague*. Trina's plotline is the first in a series of Norris's novels suggesting that, for him, a woman removed from proper nineteenth-century domesticity becomes dysfunctional. Once Trina is made into the breadwinner, McTeague becomes brutal with her, punching her "with his closed fist" and even biting her fingers, "crunching and grinding them with his immense teeth" (479). Yet, ironically, so fixed is her desire, she clings to him all the more: "In some strange, inexplicable way this brutality made Trina all the more affectionate" (479). And, once he abandons her and domesticity is no longer a viable object, Trina grows obsessed with hoarding gold coins. Her desire—unlike the women protagonists of Dreiser and his contemporaries—is anything but dynamic.

Although published a year after *McTeague*, Norris's novel *A Man's Woman*, as its title hints, would appear to be even more old-fashioned than its predecessor. And—its dog-eating dogs and dog-eating men notwithstanding—it is probably Norris's most temperate novel. That may seem a low bar, but a tragicomedy from a writer known for killing off his protagonists should make us pause. *A Man's Woman* marks a departure in Norris's writing, where he shifts from a negative to a positive depiction of the relations between the sexes—a shift, in other words, from showing how not to survive in the modern world to showing how to do so. Yet, surprisingly, his roadmap for surviving modernity does not entail embracing modern values or the modern forms of selfhood promulgated by his contemporaries.

The plot of *A Man's Woman* is simple (by Norris's standards, at least). Ward Bennett—part McTeague, part Captain Ahab—is leading an expedition to the North Pole. Anyone who has read Jack London's much-anthologized short story "To Build a Fire" (published two years after Norris's novel) can pretty well surmise how this goes: frostbite, deaths of dogs, meals of dogs, amputations, fatalities—the whole naturalist menu of arctic miseries. When Bennett and the few surviving expeditioners have all but despaired, the second-in-command, Richard Ferris, convinced that they're all done for, tells Bennett what he believes will be a white lie—that the woman he loves, Lloyd Searight, loves him back. This factitious news strengthens Bennett's resolve to live, and, through sheer force of will, he preserves the remaining men—along with the single undevoured dog—long enough for them to be rescued by a whaling ship.

Returning home a hero, Bennett seeks what he has been led to view as his just deserts, Lloyd. An heiress who has chosen to devote her life to the nursing profession, Lloyd "wanted ... to count in the general economy of things" (57). Self-assured and independent as she is, Lloyd is cursed with the same Achilles' heel as any other character in a naturalist novel—nature or, as Norris repeatedly terms it here, "the Enemy." For Bennett, the Enemy is "the titanic primal strength of a chaotic world" (5), but, for Lloyd, it is her sex, and, in Norris's essentialist vision, that means the urge to submit as a wife. What stands between Lloyd and Bennett at first seems to be the fact that she has told herself that she loves Ferris, but her determination to beat nature and retain her independence is eventually revealed as the true obstacle. Trying to beat nature in an insistently naturalist novel, we know, is a losing game, and so, "after all those years of repression, suddenly the sweet, dim thought she had hidden in her secret heart's heart had leaped to light and to articulate words" (147).

Reader, she married him. Victorian though this plot surely is, Fleissner's recent study *Maladies of the Will* saves us from overlooking what is distinctly modern about this otherwise conventional story. Although Fleissner does not discuss this particular novel, her theorization of Norris fully applies here. She persuasively demonstrates that, between the earlier nineteenth century and the Progressive Era, there was a shift in the way that the individual will was understood: "'Weakness of will' was conceived, finally, as a matter more of inertia rather than of rampaging pursuit of desires—setting the stage for the reconstrual of strong will as bodily energy rather than moral self-restraint" (276). And it is precisely a gender-inflected compatibility between the intensities of Bennett's and Lloyd's wills that so suits them for each other: "His physical strength, once so enormous, was as a reed in the woman's hand; his will, so indomitable, was as powerless as an infant's before the woman's calm resolve, rising up there before him and overmastering him at a time he believed it to be forever weakened" (241). Unlike the inert subjects that Fleissner identifies elsewhere in Norris's fiction as bad subjects, both Bennett and Lloyd are nothing if not active.

Bennett is "that indomitable man of iron whom no fortune could break nor bend, and who imposed his will . . . as it were a yoke of steel" (22). For Lloyd, "first, last, and always were acts, acts, acts—concrete, substantial, material acts" (57).

Even so, Norris in this novel ultimately presses that active Progressive-Era view of the will into the service of an essentially conservative, Victorian view of gender and selfhood. Norris has reproduced separate-spheres ideology par excellence, even if his "angel in the house" is more willful than most of her foremothers. Lloyd gives up her nursing practice to devote herself fully to wife-hood, a move the narrator greets with encomium: "Hers was the woman's part. Already she had assumed it; steadfast unselfishness, renunciation, patience, the heroism greater than all others, that sits with folded hands, quiet, unshaken, and under fearful stress, en-dures, and endures, and endures" (244). But, while this kind of stony renunciation is laudable in the wife, it is, for Norris, contemptible in the husband: "Here widened the difference between the man and the woman. Lloyd's discontinuance of her life-work had been in the nature of heroic subjugation of self. Bennett's abandonment of his career was hardly better than weakness. In the one it had been re-nunciation; in the other surrender" (242). The work the narrator has in mind for Bennett is the resumption of the arctic expedition, and, in accepting her vocation as a wife, Lloyd accepts her role as help-mate. She resolves that she must get him out of the house and back on the expedition, although she "must influence him indirectly," "a situation that called for all her feminine tact" (259–60).

As if the circumstances weren't Victorian enough, the expedition receives a patriotic cast. Precipitated by an expedition of Englishmen headed for the North Pole, the nationalistic implications first surface in Lloyd's appeal to Bennett. "Why should it not be us?" she asks him; "Why shouldn't *our* flag be the first at the Pole?" (247). Later, Bennett is visited by a group hopeful of funding an Ameri-can expedition—"American from start to finish" (272)—with him at the helm. So national an affair is this to be that even Congress had agreed to appropriate funds for it, until reports of the English ex-pedition's setbacks begin circulating. And who volunteers to make up the deficit? None other than Bennett's own wife. This is textbook "manifest domesticity"—Amy Kaplan's influential term, explained in *Anarchy of Empire*, describing the symbiotic relationship in the nineteenth century between empire and domestic ideology, man's sphere and woman's.

Of all Norris's novels, *A Man's Woman* offers possibly the clearest picture of his view of individual will. For him, outsize will outstripping its object is no better than weak will incapable of attaching to an object. Of the unreformed Bennett, the narrator explains: "He had long since passed the limit—though perhaps he did not know it himself—where he could see anything but the point he had determined to reach. . . . His furious energy, his resolve to conquer at all costs, had become at last a sort of direct frenzy. The engine he had set in motion was now beyond his control" (143). And Lloyd, we have seen, with her "stubborn energy," also has been given to an aimless willfulness of which the novel disapproves (57). But it is through the redirecting of these energies—what Fleissner might describe as the linking of these individual wills with a big Will—that they are cured of their waywardness. Lloyd throws herself into the service of her home and husband, and her doing so enables her husband to throw himself into the service of his country. Could a resolution be any more nineteenth-century?

As this brief look at two of Norris's most woman-centered fictions should demonstrate, Norris had not been in the habit of writing the kinds of female characters common among his contemporaries. As Lloyd and *McTeague*'s Trina Sieppe show, Norris could not envision the ascendancy of insatiable women, social selves with malleable desires, largely for the fact that, in his fictional worlds, he either would not or could not untether himself from a Victorian economy of desire. And his old-fashioned conception of women and desire, I am convinced, is at the root of his rearguard vision of the businessman in his last published novel, *The Pit*—to which we now turn.

In one of the most sustained twenty-first-century treatments of *The Pit*, Zimmerman interprets the novel in almost exactly the opposite way that I do. For one, seeking to establish Norris's "market plot as an artist fable" (132), Zimmerman's interpretation would lead us to conceive of *The Pit* as being far less different from Dreiser's business novel than I have been suggesting: The spheres of art and commerce, the feminine and the masculine, are presented as analogous. But that's not all. "This artist fable," Zimmerman argues, "doubles as a mesmerist tale" registering Norris's "fascination and uneasiness with new, proliferating forms of economic imitation and identification at the turn of the century" (125). On this reading, the novel is about the same kinds of malleable, adaptable subjects that we have been considering all along.

Were there such compatibility and analogy in the novel as Zimmerman suggests—between husband and wife, business and art, self and other self—we would be hard-pressed to account for the Howellsian ending of the story, predicating the moral rise of the grasping businessman on his financial fall. In short, the kind of closure we witness here is entirely out of keeping with the plot of the social self, which, as we have seen, is open-ended and allergic to the moral certitude with which Norris's novel concludes. For all his effort to position himself as the modern foil to his nineteenth-century forebears, *The Pit* is often strikingly old-fashioned. In fact, Laura is portrayed as a female Quixote, in certain ways more outdated than Charlotte Lennox's heroine by that name would have been by early-twentieth-century standards. Though trained in drama—"consumed," we're told, "with vague ambitions to be a great actress of Shakespearean rôles" (18)—she, once married, can act but one part, that of doting wife. Norris describes her condition in this way: "A great fact had entered her world, a great new element, that dwarfed all other thoughts, all other considerations. This was her love for her husband" (203).

The resemblance here to Trina Sieppe's monomaniacal obsession with her coins—"She loved her money with an intensity that she could hardly express" (*McTeague* 478)—is no accident. Laura, too, is an obsessive whose fixation is exacerbated by her husband's neglect. In Norris's framing, the overexpansion of one sphere triggers a corresponding overexpansion in the other: As Jadwin becomes ever more the man of business, Laura dives deeper into womanly domesticity. (And we might construe Trina's coin hoarding in similar terms—as an attempt to prevent money from circulating and thereby imprison commerce within the home.) Norris's description of Laura's transformation is revealing:

It was by this means that, in the end, she succeeded in fitting herself to her new surroundings. Innocently enough, and with a harmless, almost childlike, affectation, she posed a little, and by so doing found the solution of the incongruity between herself—the Laura of moderate means and quiet life—and the massive luxury with which she was now surrounded. Without knowing it, she began to act the part of a great lady—and she acted it well. She assumed the existence of her numerous servants as she assumed the fact of the trees in the park; she gave herself into the hands of her maid, not as Laura Jadwin of herself would have done it, clumsily and with the constraint of inexperience, but as she would have done it if she had been acting the part on the stage, with an air, with all the nonchalance of a marquise, with—in fine—all the superb condescension of her "grand manner." (213)

The fact that Laura, as she acclimates to her conjugal home, is fond of posing might mislead one into likening her to the malleable social selves of Norris's contemporaries. The problem with such a view is that there is no one else around to impel her self-fashioning, no audience to applaud the performance. Instead, what we find here is a solitary, two-step transformation, in which Laura, becoming the lady of the house, both merges with the home—signaling her complete identification with it—and aggrandizes herself along with it. A majestic example of the type that Quentin Anderson dubbed "the imperial self," Laura levitates out of the matrix of human relations and into the heights of domestic divinity. We see as much in the widening chasm between her and her own sister, whose name, Page, in its feudal connotations, underscores her lifelong deference to her queenly elder sibling.[12] In their final major altercation, Laura more or less exiles Page, imperiously hurling at the younger woman, "Have I got to answer to you for what I do? . . . Now I forbid it—from this day on. What I do is my affair; I'll do as I please, do you understand?" (302).

Matters only get worse for Laura as the erosion of her home continues, so much so that she envisions herself as being at war with business for the possession of her husband: "Even here, here in her home, her husband's head upon her lap, in the quiet and stillness of her hour, the distant rumble came to her ears. Somewhere, far off there in the darkness of the night, the great forces were manoeuvring for position once more. To-morrow would come the grapple, and one or the other must fall—her husband or the enemy [i.e., the wheat trade]. How keep him to herself when the great conflict impended? She knew how the thunder of the captains and the shoutings appealed to him" (315–16). Laura reaches her moral nadir—and her obsession with wifehood its apex—when she neglects the funeral of Mr. Cressler, who "was almost a second father to the parentless Dearborn girls" (16). After eyeing Mrs. Cressler's note containing the details of the funeral of her "second father," Laura displays something less than the filial piety we might expect:

> And then, her resolution girding itself, her will power at fullest stretch, she had put the tragedy from her. Other and—for her— more momentous events impended. Everything in life, even death itself, must stand aside while her love was put to the test. Life and death were little things. Love only existed; let her husband's career fail; what did it import so only love stood the strain and issued from the struggle triumphant? And now, as she lay upon her couch, she crushed down all compunction for the pitiful calamity whose last scene she had discovered, her thoughts once more upon her husband and herself. (401)

"Love only existed": In reporting Laura's deranged response to the tragedy—her unwillingness to allow mourning her second father's death to interfere with pursuing her husband's attention—Norris paraphrases Lord Byron's infamous caricature of women in *Don Juan*, wherein Byron claims that love is "woman's whole existence." (Elsewhere in the novel, Byron is referenced directly.) Laura's retreat into the domestic sphere in response to her husband's absorption by business seems complete, and, like Trina's, what a disfigurement it is.

Business disfigures Jadwin even worse. Just as the sixth chapter, the novel's inflection point, opens with his wife's transformation into the "angel in the house," so, too, does it initiate Jadwin's full immersion into business. Norris figures this immersion as a mounting addiction: It starts out small—a little here, a little there, then a little more—until the obsession with "speculating" (the era's gambling-inflected name for stock trading) consumes him. In the third chapter, Jadwin keeps a healthy skepticism toward speculating, conscious of his susceptibility to getting hooked: "That's why I said I'd keep out of it. It isn't so much the money as the fun of playing the game. With half a show, I would get in a little more and a little more, till by and by I'd try to throw a big thing, and instead, the big thing would throw me" (86–87). By the sixth chapter, however, the erstwhile cautious millionaire—once content to confine his dealings to real estate—has been "blooded to the game" (190).

Like an alcoholic acquiring a liquor store, the business-crazed Jadwin ends the chapter buying a seat on the Board of Trade. From there, his descent is steep. Despite all Laura's attempts to draw his attention back to her and their home, the call of trading is irresistible (indeed, Norris uses the idiosyncratic word *resistless* ten times in the novel, mostly after chapter 6). As Laura scolds, "You are so nervous sometimes, and sometimes you don't listen to me when I talk to you. I can just see what's in your mind. It's wheat—wheat—wheat, wheat—wheat—wheat, all the time. Oh, if you knew how I hated and feared it!" (231). With his wonted lack of subtlety, Norris makes this obsessive repetition into a thudding refrain in Jadwin's head: "In the cold, dim silence of the earliest dawn Curtis Jadwin went to bed, only to lie awake, staring up into the darkness, planning, devising new measures, reviewing the day's doings, while the faint tides of blood behind the eardrums murmured ceaselessly to the overdriven brain, 'Wheat—wheat—wheat, wheat—wheat—wheat'" (283). Leaving us in no doubt that his condition is meant to be understood as an addiction, the narrator explains, "Going to and fro in La Salle Street, or sitting in Gretry's office, where the roar of the Pit dinned forever in his ears, he could forget these strange symptoms" (348). Just as drinking quiets the alcoholic's DTs, so speculating calms Jadwin's addled mind.

The Jadwins are, like many of Norris's other characters, monomaniacs. And, if we learn nothing else from American literature's famous monomaniac—Melville's captain who sacrifices the lives of most of his crew in the pursuit of his obsession—monomaniacs are ill-equipped to be social selves (not that they would have it any other way). Unlike his contemporaries, Norris never tapped into the potential inhering in the more open-ended ways of conceiving of the self prevalent in the era. It is, as I see it, no accident, then, that he was unable (or perhaps unwilling) to get past the nineteenth century's characteristic solution for dealing with what Regenia Gagnier memorably calls "the insatiability of human wants." Although we in the twenty-first century—a time of unprecedented socioeconomic inequality in the United States and ruled by "centibillionaires"—are painfully aware that rapacious, insatiable people very often prosper, Norris maintains a vision of the world scarcely different from his predecessors', in which hubris is punished. In attempting to corner the wheat market, Jadwin is figured as "fighting against the earth itself" (347), rather than, say, as "a spider in a spangled net," "surrounded . . . in a splendid, glittering network of connections," as Dreiser's Cowperwood is described (157). Accordingly, *The Pit* ends decisively: Financially bankrupt but reconciled in love, the chastened Jadwins depart Chicago for a simpler life, in their rearview "the Board of Trade building, black, monolithic, crouching on its foundations like a monstrous sphinx with blind eyes, silent, grave" (421).

CONCLUSION

For other writers of the period, rejecting the individualistic views of selfhood so central to the nineteenth-century realist novel yielded different results. It enabled them to portray modern American culture, in all its excess and variability, more truthfully and, for the most part, dispassionately. And, notably, they were not the first cohort of writers in the English language to take women as their starting points for picturing modern life and modern selfhood. While Nancy Armstrong certainly exaggerated in claiming that the novel as a genre necessarily propagates the individual subject (her and Tennenhouse's recent work on the American novel, as I have explained, already evinces a retreat from this position), my findings about the construction of the business tycoon, predicated on the reimagining of subjectivity through reimagining women, reinforce the core argument of her earliest book. I have in mind her transformative *Desire and Domestic Fiction*, where, examining the eighteenth-century English novel, she makes the counterintuitive assertion that women were the first modern subjects—that, in other words, writers first used women as the vehicles for depicting a kind of subjectivity that was distinctly modern.

Armstrong's study helps us begin to see how central women have been to the project of defining modernity. In showing that reimagining women was prerequisite in the effort to assimilate imaginatively business's permeation of American culture, this chapter provides evidence suggesting that women very well may be prime in *all* initial efforts to grapple with new stages of modernity. Is this because, as Armstrong suggests, the customary understanding of women as private beings enables the forms of selfhood they inhabit and desire they display to seem natural, divorced from history, politics, and economics? Or is it as Fleissner intimates in *Women, Compulsion, Modernity*—that women have seemed such apt representatives of modernity because modern societies always have been aware at some level that their futures hinged on women's choices? I think they are both right.

The separate-spheres ideology that we have inherited from the Victorians, it is further clear, often obscures far more than it illuminates. Man and woman, art and business, public and private— these are dichotomies that had long been suspect but that come under intense scrutiny in the work of the second generation of American realist writers, whose liminal historical position—framed by the Civil War and the nation's frenetic phase of capitalist modernization— make them especially alive to the contradictions of modernity's sustaining myths.

The End

The Death of the American Dream and Birth of the Modernist Novel

The fascination that suffuses the depictions of women in the novels of other realist writers of this generation turns into something quite different in Booth Tarkington's 1921 novel *Alice Adams*. Tarkington's attitude toward his protagonist is, at best, "unsentimental but sympathetic," as Adam Sorkin notes in one of the few studies of the novel in the last half-century (186). However, the reasons for Tarkington's distance from Alice and for the humbling, if not humiliating, fate that he engineers for her are not as obvious as they may seem. Sorkin imputes Alice's misfortunes to Tarkington's elitism, writing, "He comfortably criticized the dirty, noisy, boorish twentieth century from the nostalgic perspective of his fond memories of the 'Golden Age' of his boyhood. Tarkington's world-view was limited and conservative" (184). But to attribute Tarkington's handling of Alice's story so cavalierly to his snobbery—to claim that, for this author, "the social and personal defeat of the protagonist is the given of her social and economic situation" (196)—glosses over the previous two decades of fiction in the United States and misses what is most innovative in the novel. As is surely apparent by now, in the first decades of the twentieth century, lowly socioeconomic beginnings were just as likely to serve as the starting points for meteoric social ascents, especially for white middle-class heroines.

Much in the narrative makes it clear that Tarkington sought to place himself in dialogue with his contemporaries, who were themselves in dialogue with the previous generation of realist writers. The most salient clue to this fact lies in his characterization of Alice. Like the other heroines we have seen, Alice is a social self, plastic and all too eager to try on the many masks proffered by an age of personality. At the very moment of her introduction, she is caught in what seems a stage rehearsal at her dressing table: "Alice had been playing with the mirror's reflections—posturing her arms and her expressions, clasping her hands behind her neck, and tilting back her head to foreshorten the face in a tableau conceived to represent sauciness, then one of scornful toleration, and all very piquant" (14). Her other-directedness and ontological instability are emphasized throughout the novel, most of all during her flirtations with Arthur Russell, her quasi-suitor. After one of Alice's prodigious displays of coquettish banter, Russell is left in awe: "Never had he seen a creature so plastic or so wistful" (147). When they begin to probe the nature of her ontology, Russell can only equivocate, replying, "I thought you were like what you *are* like" (149)—a tautological formulation that echoes Undine Spragg's "I want what others want" (61). The most "definite" answer at which they are able to arrive comes, as Alice notes, through comparing her to the moneyed Mildred Palmer. The terms of the comparison are revealing. According to Alice, Mildred is "perfect—why, she's *perfectly* perfect!" (149). It becomes clear that Tarkington is exploiting the etymology of the word *perfect* ("completed" or "thoroughly made") when Alice goes on to describe her as "some big, noble, cold statue." Whereas Mildred is—like the old-fashioned men we have seen in other novels— made and definable, Alice remains always in the making and eludes definition.

Other aspects of Alice link her to the social selves of earlier novels, such as her extraordinary social perspicacity, captured in Russell's playful insistence that she must be a "mind reader" (147). She also embodies the paradox of personality, at once willful and compulsive. Tellingly, however, this is as far as Tarkington is willing to follow his contemporaries. While he borrows from their characterizations, he departs from their plots. Through his conspicuous divergences from the prevailing patterns in the American realist fiction of his day, Tarkington registers his misgivings about the stories that his compatriots had been telling about social mobility in the United States, particularly as it relates to middle-class white women. Although Alice is an expert performer, none of her performances yields even a fraction of the social success won by her malleable predecessors. The time she treats a mundane run of errands as an occasion for a "show of fashion" is illustrative (35). She goes out dressed like the actresses and models from the magazines she reads, swinging a Malacca cane and impeded by the "closeness of her skirt" (35). That she fails in her attempt to mystify and dazzle becomes painfully apparent. As Alice passes the prim Mrs. Dowling, the elderly woman makes it "all too evident" that "the approaching gracefulness was uncongenial" (36). In addition, Tarkington skillfully euphemizes the response that she elicits from "a gentleman of forty or so," whose prurient attentions Alice mistakes for confirmation of "how wonderful, how mysterious, she was" (39). On the contrary, the narrator suggests—in what is surely one of the most genteel allusions to an erection in all of fiction—that the gentleman responds less nobly, "seeming to be preoccupied the while with problems that kept his eyes to the pavement" (37).

Tarkington continues to burlesque Alice's social performances, demonstrating the paltry uses to which she is forced to apply her charms. When she later attends Mildred Palmer's party (invited only out of pity), Alice finds herself almost entirely ignored and resorts to practicing "an art that affords but a limited variety of methods, even to the expert: the art of seeming to have an escort or partner when there is none" (111). Once she exhausts this art, she tries another tactic. Discovering a "cluster of matrons" secluded off to the side, "she now meant to present the picture of a jolly girl too much interested in these wise older women to bother about every foolish young man who asked her for a dance" (120–21). They eventually rebuff her, but, as before, her optimism is equal even to these major setbacks, for, when the last elder abandons her, she remains bent on performing, pretending that "there was something the matter with the arm of her chair" (125).

However, in both this instance and her scandalous afternoon stroll, Tarkington ultimately associates Alice with black people—in a sense, *blackens* her—in order to make the fact of her failure undeniable, even to her. This tactic is in keeping with the tendency that Stephanie Foote observes in the era's fiction to racialize the failed parvenu, who is "metaphorized by being identified with more obviously 'impossible' people excluded on more transparent grounds" (12). At Alice's request, Russell goes off in search of her brother at Mildred's party and finds him, in Walter Adams's words, "shootin' dice with those coons in the cloak-room" (126). Despite the many other embarrassments of the evening, it is this one that convinces her that the evening has been a failure. Similarly, despite the patently disapproving looks of Mrs. Dowling and others as well as the lecherous gaze of the middle-aged gentleman, she has little inkling of her impropriety until one among "a group of small coloured children" exclaims, "Lady got cane! Jeez'!" (40). Later in the novel, Alice and Russell are out for a walk and wander into a working-class neighborhood, where Alice believes they won't run into any of their acquaintances. However, they espy her brother from a distance, and he is, in another of the narrator's euphemisms, "indeed accompanied" (243). We are circuitously led to understand that the woman with him is mixed-race, described as "a thin girl who made a violent black-and-white poster of herself: black dress, black flimsy boa, black stockings, white slippers, great black hat, down upon the black eyes" (243). The narrator stops just short of extending the omnipresent "black" to her person. Yet again, Tarkington associates Alice with black people—and, in this instance, the overtones of miscegenation are at their clearest—in order to put her in her place. When they reach her front door, she voices what this most recent contretemps renders too vivid to suppress: "It's spoiled, isn't it?" (246).

The way black people, the lowest of the low in the socioeconomic hierarchy, haunt Alice leads us to the root of Tarkington's apprehensions about fictional depictions of socially mobile women in the previous two decades: the fact that they downplay the significance of social context. All the women protagonists in these earlier novels are strategically shorn of familial relations. The parents of Grant's Selma White are both dead by her story's beginning; the mother of Herrick's Milly Ridge is dead as well, and her father remains hands-off; we never meet the parents of Dreiser's Carrie Meeber, and she decisively parts with her sister early in the novel; and the parents of Wharton's Undine Spragg are hopelessly inert, merely props in their daughter's whirlwind adventure. In each case, the protagonist is unmoored of all predetermined relations and thereby enabled to enjoy boundless mobility and mutability. (The marginalization of the nuclear family in these novels also bears out James Livingston's claim in *Pragmatism, Feminism, and Democracy* that, in this period, the home loses its privileged status as the locus of social relations.) Unlike her forebears, Alice is yoked to a thick, suffocating social and familial context, and the novel takes pains to suggest that these relations matter. For example, Mrs. Adams imputes all her daughter's difficulties to the fact that "we're poor, and she hasn't any background" (70). In *Alice Adams*, trying to outrun social context is a losing game. We have already seen this principle at work in Tarkington's handling of Alice's disastrous afternoon stroll, a misstep attributable to her disregard for context. Wealthy Hollywood starlets who rouge their lips, don tight skirts, and swing Malacca canes may indeed dazzle and intrigue, but the Midwestern daughter of a clerk who does so simply scandalizes.

Tarkington implies the importance of context in all kinds of other sly ways. We have, for instance, Mrs. Palmer's retort that "a girl belongs to her family" (343) and, more figuratively, the fact that Alice's father attempts to launch a *glue* works, the smelly fumes from which seem to stick to him unshakably, just as Alice's relations stick to her. Tarkington displays this conviction most artfully in the orchestration of Alice and Arthur Russell's courtship (if we can so refer to it). The two seek to maintain their romance by warding off all outside influences. Alice obsessively implores Russell not to talk to others about her, hoping to keep the image he has of her solely within her control. "But *wouldn't* it be pleasant," she coaxes, "if two people could ever just keep themselves *to* themselves, so far as they two were concerned? I mean, if they could just manage to be friends without people talking about it, or talking to *them* about it?" (231). Though Alice is understandably the more sedulous of the two in this effort, Russell dreads external interference scarcely less than she does. Almost all of their affair is conducted in private walks and on the veranda of the Adams home. For Russell, the latter becomes a "glamorous nook, with a faint golden light falling through the glass of the closed door upon Alice, and darkness everywhere" (326).

In another significant formulation, Russell imagines the space as forming a frame insulating them from social reality: "The back of the world was the wall and closed door behind them" (326). Enabling Russell to escape the encumbrances of social context, the veranda serves as a blank canvas on which he may paint whatever Alice he wishes.

But Tarkington—at least in this novel—was too much the student of Howells to sustain this dream sequence. The hard facts of economic reality uproot the couple from their charmed veranda, pushing them toward destinies consistent with their social circumstances. Contrary to the 1935 film adaptation of the novel, the two do not marry. (Certainly, no one living in that economically depressed decade wanted to see a movie suggesting that not even Katharine Hepburn's face could improve one's fortunes.) After a disastrous dinner—rendered as skillfully as Howells's in *The Rise of Silas Lapham*—the socioeconomic context that Alice has been staving off comes crashing down on her, in a farrago of unendurable summer heat, boiled brussels sprouts, and, of course, a ceaselessly chewing hired black maid. Russell never returns and, we presume, eventually weds his cousin Mildred. And Alice takes the foreordained step of enrolling at Frincke's Business College, whose old maids, she earlier remarks, portentously "looked a little like herself" (141).

In taking the novelistic subject developed by his contemporaries and providing her with a less glamorous denouement, Tarkington gives the lie to their view that personality and social selfhood alone were powerful enough to subvert socioeconomic reality. As I suggest above, his skepticism about social mobility cannot simply be attributed to the author's elitism or conservatism. It is in keeping with a major current in the 1920s, one that shaped some of our most brilliant fiction. It was clear to many in the decade that the possibility of imagining unfettered social mobility in the United States was diminishing. In his 1925 study of American millionaires of two different generations, Pitirim Sorokin, one of the era's foremost sociologists, concluded that "the period of the de facto 'open door' for social circulation of the individuals in the United States is passing and the stage of class-differentiation with the wealthy is becoming more and more hereditary and is more and more closing its door to newcomers" (636). "American society is being transformed," he continues, "into a society with rigid classes and well-outlined class divisions." Tarkington suggests that a similar transition has occurred in his Midwestern city when Mrs. Adams attributes the family's misfortunes to Mr. Adams's failure to make good when the "town was smaller" and opportunities more available, as other men had (211).

In this regard, Tarkington anticipates the Lost Generation, who expressed similar understandings of social mobility in the era. In its opening chapter, Fitzgerald's *Gatsby* (1925) places social mobility back in the days of post–Civil War industrialization, when Nick Carraway's Scottish émigré great-uncle established the family's fortune. However, by the 1920s, the doors of the upper ranks are closed to such aspirants as Jay Gatsby, no matter how gorgeously he executes the "unbroken series of successful gestures" that constitutes personality (2). And, like Alice Adams, Gatsby is a failed parvenu who gets conspicuously racialized, associated, as Barbara Will argues, "with creole or Jewish difference" (132). A year later, Hemingway similarly checks the ambitions of his Jewish social climber Robert Cohn in *The Sun Also Rises*. And the problem of "background" that so beleaguers Alice Adams becomes even more acute in Nella Larsen's novels about mixed-race women, published at the end of the decade.

Beyond their resemblances to Tarkington, the fiction produced later in the 1920s shares other qualities with the tradition of American realism described here, qualities that help illuminate how the American novel got from Howells to Fitzgerald. As we saw in this book's introduction, midcentury critics such as Richard Chase and Charles Feidelson linked the development of modernism to the romances of the antebellum period. We are now, however, in a position to see how realist fiction contributed to that development as well. As we have seen, the fiction most representative of the second phase of realism traces a shift in the relations between the sexes and concomitant changes in traditional domesticity. In the novels published before Tarkington's, we observe—in the background of stories about insatiable, mobile women—subplots about love-starved men whose demises result from their misrecognition of modern woman. Many of the classic novels of the 1920s pull this subplot from the margins and into the center, taking the form of modernist melodramas of beset manhood.[1] Gatsby's story is about his pursuit of the American Dream through the pursuit of the American girl (aptly named Daisy, echoing Henry James's paradigmatic heroine). Thoroughly romantic in his view of her, Gatsby is ultimately used up and discarded by the woman on whom he stakes everything, left to suffer the lethal consequences of her act of manslaughter. Willa Cather's *The Professor's House* (1925) concentrates on the disenchanted Godfrey St. Peter, who is nearly driven to suicide by the acquisitive and materialistic women in his life. And Hemingway's *The Sun Also Rises*, as Mark Spilka explains, presents a world in which "men no longer command respect, and women replace their natural warmth with masculine freedom," and where "there can be no serious love" (37). That novel chronicles the devastating effects that men suffer when they misrecognize modern women.

Just a glance at these later novels suggests how vital the realist fiction produced in the century's first two decades is to the larger puzzle of American literary history. What Newton Arvin wrote of Herrick in 1935 may reasonably be extended to describe the interstitial position of the other writers of his generation: "He derives directly from his immediate predecessors, and carries the tale to a point at which young writers are taking it up without break or strain." At the same time, attending to a fuller range of the realist fiction produced in the early-twentieth century compels us to think differently about the canonical realist writers whom we think we already know. By now, it should be clear that such canonical writers as Dreiser and Wharton were far from exceptional in their attempts to reimagine both the modern subject and literary realism for a new age. On the contrary, they were participating in and helping shape one of the most salient currents in American culture.

ACKNOWLEDGMENTS

―――――――

On some level, I think I have been writing *Realism after the Individual* for about as long as I have been studying literature seriously. For that reason, my debts extend far back. They go all the way back to high school, where my AP English teacher Alfonso Correa introduced me to Kate Chopin's magnificent novel, *The Awakening*, which I have not been able to put down since. When I arrived at Washington University in St. Louis as an undergraduate, my teachers there helped me study Chopin further and introduced me to her contemporaries, most notably Edith Wharton. There Vivian Pollak (who remains unutterably dear to me) proved an exceptional guide through American literature, directing my undergraduate thesis, which was divided between Chopin and Wharton. Jessica Rosenfeld, though a medievalist, was a great inspiration to me during my years as an English major, and to her, too, I remain indebted.

In the next phase of my education, in the Department of English at the University of Pennsylvania, I was blessed with more mentors. I was fortunate to have the chance to work with two of the finest Americanists in the business, Nancy Bentley and Amy Kaplan, who pointed the way to many of the answers to the questions that I had about the turn-of-the-twentieth-century American novel—one of the strangest and most innovative episodes in the long history of the novel, as I hope this book makes clear. (One of my biggest regrets is that Amy is not here to see this book.) Wendy Steiner, writer among writers, did more than any single person in my training to prepare me to do justice to these and other writers in the clearest prose possible. (I am still learning from her.) And Jennifer Fleissner, though not ever at Penn, was then and has remained a steadfast mentor and supporter. My debt to her work is evident in the preceding pages, but here let me acknowledge her kindness and unflagging faith in this somewhat eccentric project. My debts at Penn extend almost as much horizontally as they do vertically. The friendships I developed with my fellow travelers in the PhD program were—and, in some cases, still are—sustaining. I am especially thankful to my fellow Americanists—Rachel Banner and Phillip Maciak—and other graduates from the program who have been exceptionally kind to me over the years, including David Alff, Benjy Kahan, Lucía Martínez Valdivia, Katie Price, and, chief among them, Beth Blum. I also am grateful to Penn for all the institutional support that it provided as I clumsily crafted my, ahem, *courageous* dissertation.

I owe a great deal to my current institutional home, Baruch College, City University of New York (CUNY), which provided me the stability and resources that I needed to finish this book. It also gave me some of the most supportive and generous colleagues a beginning assistant professor could wish for. I am grateful for just about all my colleagues here, but a few merit special mention. For their enduring camaraderie, conviviality, and support, I thank Lisa Blankenship, Allison Deutermann, Matthew Eatough, Shelly Eversley, and Mary McGlynn. Timothy Aubry has been something like a big brother to me. When I first arrived at Baruch College, Tim took me on as a mentee and was chair for the duration of the time I was finishing this book. I'm grateful to Tim for the personal and professional advice he's been so generous with, not least of all his astute comments, at the eleventh hour, on chapter 4. I'd also like to thank a few important institutional entities for their support: the Dean's Office of the Weissman School of Arts and Sciences, Baruch College's Provost Office, PSC-CUNY, and CUNY's Faculty Fellowship Publication Program.

Beyond Baruch College, I have profited from encouragement, advice, and friendship from a number of kind souls—so many that

I am bound to forget some (for which, my apologies in advance). My sincerest thanks to Ulrich ("Uli") Baer, Pardis Dabashi, Devin Garofalo, Melissa Girard, John Havard, William J. Maxwell, Deborah McDowell, Elizabeth Miller, Joseph Rezek, Jordan Stein, and Nathan Wolff.

I acknowledge my professional debts first only in deference to the norms of the "Acknowledgments" genre, but my personal debts are no less consequential. My thanks first to my very best friend in the world, Tom Giarla, who has put up with me (and this book) for over two decades with preternatural patience. Like Tom, Nathan Watters has consistently been a boon to me, more family than friend. If space and time weren't limited, I'd spell out what the following people have meant to me, but may this list serve as a token of my gratitude, however inadequate it is. Lacey Baradel, Scott De Orio, Kristen Faeth, Sean Fagan, Jessica Fischer, Craig ("CJ") Hatch, Taylor Haywood, Sarah Lageson, Benjamin Lee, Rickey Logan, Elliot Manuel, Jacquelyn Morrison, David Ricaud, Ryan Roark, Joe Sengoba, Jonathan Shelley, Lèr Simoneaux, Abigail Skofield, Marco Valera, Rachel Westerfield, and William ("Billy") Wieczorek.

I'd like to thank the University of Chicago Press, and especially Alan Thomas, for believing in the project and for being the picture of publishing professionalism that all writers deserve. Elizabeth Ellingboe was an ideal copy editor, the most thorough I've ever had. Chicago has published the majority of the books that I most admire in literary studies. It is an honor to have mine among them.

The last and most important debt I must acknowledge is that to my grandmother, Mary Warren, who quieted the ground beneath my feet for long enough for me to catch my bearings in life and who was my first and proudest cheerleader. To her I dedicate this book.

A version of chapter 1 first appeared as "Kate Chopin and the Dilemma of Individualism," in *Kate Chopin in Context: New Approaches*, ed. Heather Ostman and Kate O'Donoghue (Palgrave Macmillan, 2015); portions of chapter 2 and the coda were published as "The Second Phase of Realism in American Fiction: The Rise and Fall of the Social Self," *Studies in the Novel* 49, no. 4 (Winter 2017): 493–517, copyright © 2017 Johns Hopkins University Press and University of North Texas; and portions of chapter 3 first appeared as "The Bildungsroman after Individualism: Ellen Glasgow's Communitarian Alternative" in *Genre: Forms of Discourse and Culture* 49, no. 3 (2016): 385–405, reprinted by permission of Duke University Press. I thank these venues both for their initial suggestions for revision and for their permission to reprint the material here.

INTRODUCTION

1. Studies that have attempted to theorize the American realist novel include Warner Berthoff's *The Ferment of Realism* (1965), Donald Pizer's *Realism and Naturalism in Nineteenth-Century American Literature* (1966), Jay Martin's *Harvests of Change* (1967), and Edwin Harrison Cady's *The Light of Common Day* (1971). Admirable though these studies are, none has had the influence on American literature that the romance thesis has or that Watt's *The Rise of the Novel* has had on scholarship on the English novel.

2. Michael Elliot has discussed the erroneous confinement of realism to Howells as well, though he is concerned with Howells's contemporaries, not with the realists of the next generation. Referring to such writers as Henry James, Mark Twain, and Sarah Orne Jewett, Elliot notes, "literary historians rarely address those figures as advocates for realism itself" (289).

3. As Michael Davitt Bell succinctly points out, "It is a virtual axiom of our literary history that during the 1890s realism in American fiction gave way to naturalism" (109).

4. Although this letter was published anonymously, Robert Rowlette makes a persuasive case for attributing it to Booth Tarkington in "Tarkington in Defense of Howells and Realism."

5. Against the common wisdom that ignorance is bliss, modernist writers placed great value in self-awareness, even of the tragic sort. T. S. Eliot was exemplary in this regard. There is, of course, the third section of *The Waste Land*, in which Tiresias, the blind seer, emerges as

the poem's paragon, the only character in the work aware of his own blindness and, ipso facto, superior to the rest. In the final section, we have the Fisher King's famous admission of the failure of his kingdom, an admission that, surprisingly, acts as consolation—"These fragments I have shored against my ruins" (69). And Eliot could appreciate tragic self-knowledge even in earlier, non-modernist writing. Of Mark Twain's *Adventures of Huckleberry Finn*—which Eliot admired—he writes, "Huck is passive and impassive, apparently always the victim of events; and yet, in his acceptance of his world and of what it does to him and others, he is more powerful than his world, because he is more *aware* than any other person in it" ("Introduction" 350; emphasis Eliot's).

6. In their journal, the Goncourt brothers record Zola saying, "I consider the word *Naturalism* as ridiculous as you do, but I shall go on repeating it over and over again, because you have to give things new names for the public to think that they are new," describing his articles on naturalism as "just so much charlatanism to puff my books" (qtd. in Link 9).

CHAPTER ONE

1. Bentley argues that Chopin's fiction overturns the more analytical, almost scientific literary realism practiced by earlier male novelists (such as Howells) in favor of a more fantastical realism attuned to "desire and bodily pleasure" (*Frantic* 145). Accordingly, Bentley construes the gentleman's inability to understand Mrs. Sommers as Chopin's way of exposing the inadequacy of a purely analytical literary realism.

2. We find a similar fixation on the novel's mythic dimension in Cristina Giorcelli's study of *The Awakening*. "In a very unobtrusive and apparently unconscious manner," she claims, "Chopin appears to have seized upon mythic figures to help unravel both the complexity and the mystery of human existence" (127).

3. For a more extended treatment of liberal individualism, see Steven Lukes's *Individualism* (1973). For examinations of liberal individualism in fiction specifically, see Gillian Brown's *Domestic Individualism* (1990), Nancy Armstrong's *How Novels Think* (2005), and Elaine Hadley's *Living Liberalism* (2010).

4. It is worth repeating Wai Chee Dimock's observation that, just nine years before the publication of *The Awakening*, Louis D. Brandeis and Samuel D. Warren had published "The Right to Privacy," "an essay arguing for 'the right of the individual to be let alone'" (*Residues* 192). Dimock's legalistic interpretation—which situates the

novel within the prevailing rights-based paradigm of the nineteenth century—bears certain resemblances to my own understanding of the novel. But our differences are significant. In Dimock's discussion, Edna's gender would appear unimportant, but I see it as paramount. Moreover, Dimock joins a host of other critics of the novel who erroneously align Chopin's views with Edna's. In suggesting that "*The Awakening* . . . would seem to embody the language of rights up to the last," Dimock neglects the dismissal of liberal individualism that Chopin enacts through killing off her heroine (221).

5. Mary Biggs and a few other critics have taken Chopin's masculinization of Edna as evidence that the heroine is queer. I do not share this perspective because I believe that it—like all interpretations that fixate on sex—places undue emphasis on Edna's choice of love object. Near the end, the narrator states plainly that "there was no one thing in the world that she desired" (654).

6. Artistry for Edna means something completely different from what it means to Adèle. The latter "was keeping up her music on account of the children" and "because she and her husband both considered it a means of brightening the home and making it attractive" (547). However, individualist that she is, Edna expresses more self-serving reasons for practicing art: "I believe I ought to work again. I feel as if I wanted to be doing something" (584). Moreover, in her isolation from the group—her refusal to sacrifice her individuality for fusion with the female community—Edna clings to what political philosopher Norman Barry refers to as "that 'separateness' and 'identity' of individual persons that is at the heart of the libertarian ethic" (20).

7. According to one of the fathers of classical liberalism, John Locke, "Though the Earth, and all inferior Creatures be common to all Men, yet every Man has a *Property* in his own *Person*. This no Body has any Right to but himself" (287).

8. In the words of a contemporary economist, quoted in the introduction, the period witnessed the "regress of self-sufficiency and the progress of association."

9. For different variations of this position on the novel, see Sandra M. Gilbert's "The Second Coming of Aphrodite" and Anca Parvalescu's "To Die Laughing and to Laugh at Dying."

CHAPTER TWO

1. See Wharton's essay "The Great American Novel" (153).

2. The Old Testament calls for the consumption of unleavened bread to commemorate the Israelites' hasty retreat from bondage in Egypt (Zeitlin 46).

3. In *The Mediating Nation*, Nathaniel Cadle points out yet another way in which pragmatist ideas about selfhood shaped realist fiction. He suggests that the pragmatist conception of the self as relational intersects with the widespread understanding of internationalism—an understanding that, according to Cadle, informed the work of realist writers. While Cadle is concerned with how this relational thinking influenced Americans' views of their relation to the rest of the world, I am concerned with how this thinking influenced their views of their relations to one another.

4. According to Fleissner, "As Carrie moves toward supporting herself, she becomes less and less imaginable as a sentimental type, and Hurstwood, left behind, grows more so" (*Women, Compulsion, Modernity* 172).

5. In Bowlby's widely cited *Just Looking*, she suggests, "Consumer culture transforms the narcissistic mirror into a shop window, the *glass* which reflects an idealized image of the woman (or man) who stands before it, in the form of the model she could buy or become" (32).

6. Among scholars of consumer culture, none has done more than Rita Felski to demonstrate how the rise of consumer culture placed women at the center of modernity. Like most historians of consumer culture, however, she renders the scene of consumption as a deeply solitary and solipsistic affair: "What is desired," she writes in typical fashion, "is not the object per se, but the imaginary gratifications with which it is invested by the fantasizing subject" (78). More so than most, Lauren Berlant seems attuned to the deeply social quality of women's fantasy in consumer culture, noting that "the gender-marked texts of women's popular culture cultivate fantasies of vague belonging as an alleviation of what is hard to manage in the lived real—social antagonisms, exploitation, compromised intimacies, the attrition of life." "Utopianism," Berlant continues, "is in the air, but one of the main utopias is normativity itself, here a felt condition of general belonging and an aspirational site of rest and recognition in and by a social world" (5). Berlant makes it clear that feminine fantasy, no matter how solipsistic or detached it may seem, is rooted in the need for belonging, just as the interminable social adjustments of pragmatist social self are.

7. For good reason, this remains the standard view of development in the nineteenth-century realist novel. Franco Moretti's and Nancy Armstrong's remarks on this subject are representative. According to Moretti, "It is not sufficient for modern bourgeois society simply to subdue the drives that oppose the standards of 'normality.' It is also necessary that, as a 'free individual,' not as a fearful subject but

as a convinced citizen, one perceives the social norms as *one's own*" (16). Armstrong puts the matter even more forcefully: "Victorian fiction is out to convince us that partial gratification is preferable to a social alternative that indulges what is presumed to be man's unlimited appetite for more" (*How Novels Think* 138).

8. Modernist fiction has long been distinguished in part by its antidevelopmental trajectories—by the way in which it, in Jed Esty's words, "resists the tyranny of plot" (2).

9. See Wolff, *A Feast of Words*, and Gilbert and Gubar's chapter on Edith Wharton in *No Man's Land*, vol. 2.

10. Fifteen years after publishing "The Real Thing," James, in *The American Scene*, would disparage more forcefully the deterioration (rather than the underdevelopment) of American culture. As Bill Brown suggests, *The American Scene* "emphasizes the extent to which the problem isn't really the not made ... but the unmade: the pulled out, the abolished, the eliminated" (181).

11. In an attempt to upend the view of naturalism as simply deterministic, Fleissner proposes the concept of compulsion, which, she suggests, "has the potential to name an understanding of agency in which individual will and its subjection to rationalizing 'forces' appear as deeply intertwined" (*Women, Compulsion, Modernity* 9).

12. On its first page, *Sister Carrie* posits the two paths that traditionally had been available to urban-bound women characters (paths that his and other novels of the time renounce): "When a girl leaves her home at eighteen, she does one of two things. Either she falls into saving hands and becomes better, or she rapidly assumes the cosmopolitan standard of virtue and becomes worse" (1).

13. In *Frantic Panoramas*, Bentley argues that "the era's most important structural development" was "the uneven, conflicted intersection of the bourgeois public sphere with the emergent publics (such as cinema, consumer cultures, and mass publications) made possible through mass-mediated communication and industry" (5).

14. I say more about James's musings below. For Simmel's remarks on this feature of modern life, see "The Metropolis and Mental Life," 337. For a postmodernist perspective, see Fredric Jameson's *Postmodernism*, 38–39.

15. According to Showalter, Moffatt is Undine's "male self" ("Spragg" 90).

CHAPTER THREE

1. See, for instance, Jed Esty's *Unseasonable Youth* and Joseph Slaughter's *Human Rights, Inc.*

2. So much energy has gone into demonstrating that the Bildungs-roman is more the academy's creation than authors', that I am nearly dissuaded from using the term. (For a good discussion of the reasons for the invention of the Bildungsroman in Europe, see Marc Redfield's *Phantom Formations*.) However, because *Bildungsroman* remains so entrenched and recognizable a term in the discipline's lexicon, anything I sacrifice in precision is compensated by gains in communicability.

3. As Nevius reports, "For weeks after its publication *Together* was discussed in the editorial and feature columns, debated in forums, and denounced in the churches. Many libraries refused to purchase it; in Canada it was banned" (166). One reviewer called it an "'an outrageous attack on American womanhood.'" And one of Herrick's students "amusedly recalls that on the Chicago campus he was known 'as that Perfectly AWFUL Man who wrote about s-x'" and characterizes *Together* as the *Lolita* of its day (Nevius 166–67). I cannot treat *Together* at length here, but I can assure readers that, compared to most of Frank Norris's oeuvre, *Together* is G-rated.

4. According to Nevius, "Will Payne, one of Herrick's most outspoken critics among his friends, complained of this forced reconciliation [between the Lanes]. 'When you show how it is,' he wrote Herrick, 'I am captivated; when you show me how it ought to be, I have doubts'" (189).

5. The interminability of desire in Mead's social self—along with its oscillation between object and subject—links it to the divided self emerging in Walter Benn Michaels's study of turn-of-the-century US fiction. Michaels suggests that US culture at the turn of the century conformed to a distinct economic logic predicated upon internal difference, the expression of "the gold standard." "What you are is what you want, in other words, what you aren't," claims Michaels, which means that, in consumer capitalist society, to stop wanting is essentially to stop being—"the sign of incipient failure, decay, and finally death" (42). I draw on Mead's social self rather than Michaels's internally schismatic self because Mead's conception, premised upon the associative turn that life had taken near the twentieth century, posits desire as the product of the social world, of associated life. This social view of desire seems to comport better with Milly's protean desire, whose vagaries are always the result of real or imagined encounters with the social world.

6. According to Faderman, "'Lesbian' describes a relationship in which two women's strongest emotions and affections are directed toward each other. Sexual contact may be a part of the relationship to a greater or lesser degree, or it may be entirely absent" (17–18).

7. In Nathaniel Hawthorne's *The Blithedale Romance* and Henry James's *The Bostonians*, for instance, Rohy finds a "celebration of the heterosexual romance as self-evident social reality [that] requires the representation of lesbian figures on whom are projected the failures or impossibilities of both literary and sexual ideologies" (11). I have difficulty crediting this conception of Hawthorne's and James's novels (especially in light of Faderman's cogent interpretation of *The Bostonians*, which Rohy does not address, as well as her biographically based speculations about James's views on lesbianism [190–97]).

8. Given historical treatments of the New Woman, Herrick's understanding of this figure as obsolete seems remarkably prescient. According to the historian Carroll Smith-Rosenberg, in the twentieth century, the focus of New Women had shifted from financial autonomy and overall independence to sexual liberation (254–57).

9. One might reasonably object to my use of the word *wedlock* to characterize this same-sex union, but I am simply following Herrick's lead. As his chapter's title, "Milly's New Marriage," suggests, he wishes us to view this union as containing all the potential for fulfillment that heterosexual marriage does so that we understand Milly's abandonment of it as an expression of her life's fundamental incompatibility with closure.

10. Recall that the social self constantly shuttles between subject and object: from an object at which the world gazes to a subject who sees that object (who sees through "the world's eyes," we might say) to a new subject modeled after the world's vision of how that object *should* look.

11. In a lofty disquisition on the impoverished state of American marriages, *The Custom of the Country*'s Mr. Bowen asserts that the American woman is the "monstrously perfect result of the system: the completest proof of its triumph" (127).

12. As the following quotation makes clear, Glasgow conceived of her Virginia-based novels as a multivolume history of Southern manners: "*The Battle Ground*, published in 1902, is the first of a series of novels which composes, in the more freely interpretative form of fiction, a social history of Virginia from the decade before the Confederacy" (*A Certain Measure* 3). For a perceptive study of the ethnographic function of realism, see Nancy Bentley's *The Ethnography of Manners*.

13. In the preface, Hardy refers to the plot of *Tess* as "one wherein the great campaign of the heroine begins after an event in her experience which has usually been treated as fatal to her part of protagonist" (4).

14. This point has been lost on critics who overemphasize Jason's role in Dorinda's development. For example, viewing Jason as "the most important person in her adult life—perhaps in her entire life," Julius Rowan Raper arrives at the erroneous conclusion that "he was the target of her lifelong project of revenge" (158). As we see in the novel's revision of *Tess*, however, it rejects revenge very early on.

15. A reviewer from *The Literary World* calls the latter half of the novel "melodramatic and devoid of sincerity" and "tawdry and unreal" (23). Her most evenhanded reviewer, from *The Daily Eagle* calls the dialogue "stagy and unnatural" and opines that Glasgow's "story shows more of that knowledge of human life which is a part of the lore of books than of that deeper knowledge which comes from the great book of human nature" (26–27). And a reviewer from the London branch of *Bookman* complains of the novel, "There is no grip of life in it..." (30). The reviews are all from Dorothy Scura's collection in *Ellen Glasgow: The Contemporary Reviews*.

16. In an essay on Glasgow's final two novels, *Beyond Defeat* (1941) and *In This Our Life* (1966), Helen Fiddyment Levy argues that, in contrast to *Barren Ground*, "*Beyond Defeat* suggests that Glasgow at last found refuge in a visionary pastoral home place presided over by an elder wise woman, an American icon" (221). However, as the remainder of my analysis makes clear, Levy's description of *Beyond Defeat* is no less applicable to *Barren Ground*.

17. Though this plot development is entirely consistent with *Barren Ground*'s aims, Glasgow's choice to have a man killed by his chivalry is somewhat surprising in light of a remark in which she seems to distance herself from the tendencies in postwar fiction associated with "male disillusionment with virtue." In *A Certain Measure*, she writes, "At all events, after the War, male disillusionment with virtue, which had thickened like dust, invaded the whole flattened area of modern prose fiction. By some ironic reversal of the situation, woman, for so long the ideal of man, became, in a literary sense, the obstacle to all his higher activities" (233).

18. A number of feminist critics, including Adrienne Rich and Elizabeth Schultz, charge Glasgow with what Elizabeth Ammons terms "benevolent racism" for her alleged failure to recognize "the tremendous imbalance of power built into the completely unequal relationship" between Dorinda and Fluvanna (Ammons qtd. in Matthews 161). Pamela Matthews gainsays this position, suggesting that Glasgow portrays the imbalance between the two women as an "inherited" obstacle that they must work together to overcome. Matthews's stance is consonant with my own understanding of the novel, for it

implies Glasgow's conviction that the pursuit of the good requires one to start from one's inherited associations, to embrace those with whom one's history is intertwined. For condemnations of Glasgow's racism, see Rich's poem "Education of a Novelist" (in her collection *The Fact of a Doorframe*); Elizabeth Schultz, "Out of the Woods and into the World"; and Elizabeth Ammons, *Conflicting Stories*.

19. MacIntyre's use of the word *narrative* to characterize his anti-individualist version of selfhood has subjected his study to misinterpretation, most notably in the otherwise canny work of philosopher Galen Strawson. In "Against Narrativity" and again in a more recent article, Strawson groups MacIntyre with subscribers to the "narrative self-constitution thesis"—thinkers, ranging from psychologists to philosophers, who claim, in the words of one exponent, that "beginning in late adolescence and young adulthood, we construct integrative narratives of the self that selectively recall the past and wishfully anticipate the future to provide our lives with some semblance of unity, purpose, and identity" (qtd. in "'We Live beyond Any Tale'" 77). Yet MacIntyre is unconcerned with the arbitrary, somewhat solipsistic stories we may tell ourselves about ourselves in order to construct a coherent sense of identity and might be better understood as taking a position completely opposite to the group with whom Strawson would classify him.

20. I borrow this phrase from James Livingston, who argues that the pragmatists and feminists of the early-twentieth century sought change in a fashion that would "annul and preserve" the past. For him, this approach "protect[s] us against the blind and unforgiving faiths of those who have exiled themselves from the present in the name of an illustrious past or a glorious future" (*Pragmatism* 12).

CHAPTER FOUR

1. Wolff ("Lily Bart"), Showalter ("The Death of the Lady (Novelist)" 139), Steiner ("The Causes of Effect" 280), Gilbert and Gubar (138), and Fedorko (477) are only a few of the many critics to have discussed the aesthetic implications of Lily's name.

2. After writing *The American* (1877), James confesses in the preface for the 1907 edition by Charles Scribner's Sons that he had been more "romantic" than realistic in having the aristocratic Mademoiselle Bellegarde reject his millionaire American, Christopher Newman. Had he permitted the story to be controlled by "our general sense of 'the way things happen,'" James writes, the "Bellegardes would positively have jumped ... at my rich and easy American" (xviii, xix).

3. Poe's "The Purloined Letter" is nothing if not a spirited defense of the value of poetic reasoning in favor of quantitative reasoning, an outgrowth of the cultural elite's anxiety about the vulgarization of the American mind amid the rise of industry. For example, over the course of Monsieur Dupin's lengthy, exuberant defense of poetic reasoning, after he alone is able to crack the mystery of the purloined letter, Dupin pointedly asks, "What is true of *relation*—of form and quantity—is often grossly false in regard to morals . . ." (695).

4. Dreiser was fond of anachronism. In his essay "The American Financier," for example, he refers to Cosimo de' Medici as "little more than a very active Vanderbilt I"—as if the Italian banker hadn't preceded the American industrialist by more than three centuries (76)!

5. There is compelling evidence suggesting that Dreiser knew full well that, in applying the discourse of personality to antebellum culture, he was being anachronistic. In his essay titled "Personality," for instance, he alludes to the growing ascendancy of personality over character, writing,

> It is significant of the intellectual development of America, if not of other countries, that we hear less these days of *character*, that something or somewhat which we were all supposed to have, or at least develop for ourselves or make (!) à la Washington, Lincoln, Grant, etc., who in most American schoolbook essays and college addresses were and still are supposed to have *made* their skill, endurance, resourcefulness, etc.; and more of that other thing which we call personality and which for a long time apparently we were not supposed to have, that unexplainable, inescapable something with which we come and in which even here in America we are now beginning to believe. (109)

6. According to Zimmerman, "Accounting provides the medium and idiom in which Cowperwood's fight for survival is carried out. This focus marks *The Financier*'s difference from Dreiser's earlier published novels, *Sister Carrie* (1900) and *Jennie Gerhardt* (1911) . . ." (195).

7. Here is Michaels:

> I should like to suggest here that Carrie's economy of desire involves an unequivocal endorsement of what many of Dreiser's contemporaries, most of his successors, and finally Dreiser himself regarded as the greatest of all social and economic evils, the unrestrained capitalism of the late nineteenth and early twentieth centuries. The power of *Sister Carrie*, then, arguably the greatest American realist novel, derives not from its scathing

"picture" of capitalist "conditions" but from its unabashed and extraordinarily literal acceptance of the economy that produced those conditions. (35)

8. Carl S. Smith develops Dreiser's equation of businessman and artist at length, observing, for example, that "Dreiser begins to blur the distinctions between the Cowperwoods and the Rosettis of this world" (152).

9. According to Gillian Brown, "Nineteenth-century American individualism takes on its peculiarly 'individualistic' properties as domesticity inflects it with values of interiority, privacy, and psychology" (1).

10. In light of the unorthodox view of sexual morality expressed here, one wonders somewhat at Leslie Fiedler's severe, if amusing, construction of Dreiser as a prig. "Dreiser," writes Fiedler, "came of the kind of people who copulate in the dark and live out their lives without ever seeing their sexual partners nude; and he was brought up on the kind of book which made it impossible for him to write convincingly about the act of love; his subject was, like theirs, when erotic at all, the traditional 'consequences of seduction'" (250).

11. Norris's antipathy toward Howells's realism is well known, expressed most explicitly in his essay "A Plea for Romantic Fiction." Caricaturing his predecessor's work as genteel, Norris there implies that Howells's plots turned on little more than "the drama of a broken teacup" (560). He criticizes Howells in *The Pit* as well, even if indirectly. To underscore his heroine's prudishness, he writes, "The novelists of the day she ignored almost completely, and voluntarily. Only occasionally, and then as a concession, she permitted herself a reading of Mr. Howells" (42). And Jadwin, her husband and male counterpart, admires him too, explaining, "'Nothing much happens . . . But I *know* all those people'" (216). These are indications that Norris did not view these as artistic people, and they further undermine Zimmerman's interpretation of the novel as "an artist fable," an interpretation I discuss in greater detail below.

12. Given the great divide between my interpretation and Zimmerman's, it will come as no surprise that he interprets Page's name differently. He writes, "Her name is no accident, then, since she represents the only way to read the unreadable. We read her reading the panic, and we read her reading Jadwin's failure without comprehending it. Page thus stands in, finally, for the pages of Norris's book that must, in the end, fail to comprehend the panic in order to move us forward without our becoming mesmerized" (147–48). But, as I have

explained, I do not see *The Pit* as focusing in any significant measure on mesmerism. Furthermore, in light of the novel's repeated recurrence to Laura's "grand manner"—not to mention her very name and the laurels she pursues—we have yet more cause to construe the younger sister's name as a reference to a subordinate rather than a sheet of paper.

CODA

1. I am adapting this phrase from the title of Nina Baym's influential essay "Melodramas of Beset Manhood." Though Baym concentrates on literature from the antebellum period, American writers of the 1920s replay a number of the misogynistic themes that she notes in the literature of and scholarship about that earlier historical moment. Little wonder, since the myth-and-symbol critical approach that Baym criticizes emerged largely in response to the aesthetics of modernism.

WORKS CITED

Ammons, Elizabeth. *Conflicting Stories: American Women Writers at the Turn into the Twentieth Century.* Oxford University Press, 1991.

Anderson, Quentin. *The Imperial Self: An Essay in American Literary and Cultural History.* Knopf, 1971.

Armstrong, Nancy. *Desire and Domestic Fiction: A Political History of the Novel.* Oxford University Press, 1987.

Armstrong, Nancy. *How Novels Think: The Limits of Individualism from 1719–1900.* Columbia University Press, 2005.

Armstrong, Nancy, and Leonard Tennenhouse. *Novels in the Time of Democratic Writing: The American Example.* University of Pennsylvania Press, 2018.

Arvin, Newton. "Homage to Robert Herrick." *New Republic*, March 5, 1935. http://www.newrepublic.com/book/review/homage-robert-herrick.

Barry, Norman. *On Classical Liberalism and Libertarianism.* St. Martin's, 1987.

Baudrillard, Jean. "The Precession of the Simulacrum." In *The Norton Anthology of Theory and Criticism*, edited by Vincent Leitch et al. 1st ed. W. W. Norton, 2001.

Baym, Nina. "Melodramas of Beset Manhood: How Theories of American Fiction Exclude Women Authors." *American Quarterly* 33, no. 2 (Summer 1981): 123–39.

Beard, George Miller. *American Nervousness, Its Causes and Consequences.* Arno Press and The New York Times, 1972.

Bell, Michael Davitt. *The Problem of American Realism: Studies in the Cultural History of an Idea*. University of Chicago Press, 1993.

Bentley, Nancy. *The Ethnography of Manners: Hawthorne, James, Wharton*. Cambridge University Press, 1995.

Bentley, Nancy. *Frantic Panoramas: American Literature and Mass Culture, 1870–1920*. University of Pennsylvania Press, 2009.

Berlant, Lauren. *The Female Complaint: The Unfinished Business of Sentimentality in American Culture*. Duke University Press, 2008.

Berthoff, Warner. *The Ferment of Realism: American Literature, 1884–1919*. Free Press, 1965.

Biggs, Mary. "'Si tu Savais': The Gay/Transgendered Sensibility of Kate Chopin's *The Awakening*." *Women's Studies* 33 (2004): 145–81.

Birnbaum, Michele A. "'Alien Hands': Kate Chopin and the Colonization of Race." *American Literature* 66, no. 2 (1994): 301–23.

Bloom, Harold. *Genius: A Mosaic of One Hundred Exemplary Creative Minds*. Warner Books, 2002.

Bowlby, Rachel. *Just Looking: Consumer Culture in Dreiser, Gissing, and Zola*. Methuen, 1985.

Brown, Bill. *A Sense of Things: The Object Matter of American Literature*. University of Chicago Press, 2003.

Brown, Gillian. *Domestic Individualism: Imagining Self in Nineteenth-Century America*. University of California Press, 1990.

Buckley, Jerome H. *Season of Youth: The Bildungsroman from Dickens to Golding*. Harvard University Press, 1974.

Cadle, Nathaniel. *The Mediating Nation: Late American Realism, Globalization, and the Progressive State*. University of North Carolina Press, 2014.

Cady, Edwin Harrison. *The Light of Common Day: Realism in American Fiction*. Indiana University Press, 1971.

Campbell, Donna. "*At Fault*: A Reappraisal of Kate Chopin's Other Novel." In *The Cambridge Companion to Kate Chopin*, edited by Janet Beer, 27–43. Cambridge University Press, 2008.

Campbell, Donna. "'Where Are the Ladies?' Wharton, Glasgow, and American Women Naturalists." *Studies in American Naturalism* 1, nos. 1 & 2 (2006): 152–69.

Cather, Willa. *The Professor's House*. Vintage Books, 1990.

Chase, Richard. *The American Novel and Its Tradition*. Doubleday, 1957.

Chopin, Kate. *At Fault*. In Gilbert, *Kate Chopin*, 1–159.

Chopin, Kate. *The Awakening*. In Gilbert, *Kate Chopin*, 519–655.

Chopin, Kate. "An Egyptian Cigarette." In Gilbert, *Kate Chopin*, 894–97.

Chopin, Kate. "Emancipation: A Life Fable." In Gilbert, *Kate Chopin*, 659.

Chopin, Kate. *Kate Chopin: Complete Novels and Stories*, edited by Sandra M. Gilbert. New Library of America, 2002.

Chopin, Kate. "Miss Witherwell's Mistake." In Gilbert, *Kate Chopin*, 683–91.

Chopin, Kate. "A Pair of Silk Stockings." In Gilbert, *Kate Chopin*, 816–20.

Chopin, Kate. "The Storm." In Gilbert, *Kate Chopin*, 926–31.

Dabashi, Pardis. *Losing the Plot: Film and Feeling in the Modern Novel*. University of Chicago Press, 2023.

Delbanco, Andrew. "The Half-Life of Edna Pontellier." In *New Essays on The Awakening*, edited by Wendy Martin, 89–107. Cambridge University Press, 1988.

Dewey, John. "School Conditions and the Training of Thought." In *Pragmatism Old and New: Selected Writings*, edited by Susan Haack, 331–40. Prometheus Books, 2006.

Dimock, Wai Chee. "Debasing Exchange: Edith Wharton's *The House of Mirth*." *PMLA* 100, no. 5 (1985): 783–92.

Dimock, Wai Chee. *Residues of Justice: Literature, Law, Philosophy*. University of California Press, 1997.

Dreiser, Theodore. "The American Financier." In *Hey Rub-a-Dub-Dub: A Book of the Mystery and Wonder and Terror of Life*, 74–92. Boni and Liveright, 1920.

Dreiser, Theodore. *The Financier*. In *Trilogy of Desire: Three Novels by Theodore Dreiser*, 1–503. World Publishing, 1972.

Dreiser, Theodore. "Personality." In *Hey Rub-a-Dub-Dub: A Book of the Mystery and Wonder and Terror of Life*, 107–15. Boni and Liveright, 1920.

Dreiser, Theodore. *Sister Carrie*. Edited by Donald Pizer. W. W. Norton, 2006.

Eble, Kenneth. "A Forgotten Novel." In *Kate Chopin*, edited by Harold Bloom, 7–16. Chelsea House Publishers, 1987.

Edelman, Lee. *No Future: Queer Theory and the Death Drive*. Duke University Press, 2004.

Eliot, T. S. "Introduction to *Adventures of Huckleberry Finn*." In *Adventures of Huckleberry Finn*, edited by Thomas Cooley, 348–54. W. W. Norton, 1999.

Eliot, T. S. "Tradition and the Individual Talent." In *The Norton Anthology of Theory and Criticism*, edited by Vincent Leitch et al., 1092–98. W. W. Norton, 2001.

Eliot, T. S. *"The Waste Land" and Other Poems*. Edited by Frank Kermode. Penguin, 1998.

Elliot, Michael. "Realism and Radicalism: The School of Howells." In *The Cambridge History of the American Novel*, edited by Leonard Cassuto,

Clare Virgina Eby, and Benjamin Reiss, 289–303. Cambridge University Press, 2011.

Emerson, Ralph Waldo. "Friendship." In *Essays and Lectures*, edited by Joel Porte, 339–54. The Library of America, 1983.

Esty, Jed. *Unseasonable Youth: Modernism, Colonialism, and the Fiction of Development*. Oxford University Press, 2011.

Evans, Brad. "Realism *as* Modernism." In *The Oxford Handbook of American Literary Realism*, edited by Keith Newlin, 139–62. Oxford University Press, 2019.

Faderman, Lillian. *Surpassing the Love of Men: Romantic Friendship and Love between Women, from the Renaissance to the Present*. 1st ed. Morrow, 1981.

Fedorko, Kathy. "Lily's Story: Edith Wharton's *House of Mirth*." In *A Companion to the American Novel*, 475–87. Wiley Blackwood, 2012.

Feidelson, Charles. *Symbolism and American Literature*. University of Chicago Press, 1953.

Felski, Rita. *The Gender of Modernity*. Harvard University Press, 1995.

Fiedler, Leslie A. *Love and Death in the American Novel*. Dalkey Archive Press, 1960.

Fitzgerald, F. Scott. *The Great Gatsby*. Simon & Schuster, 2003.

Flax, Jane. *Thinking Fragments: Psychoanalysis, Feminism, and Postmodernism in the Contemporary West*. University of California Press, 1990.

Fleissner, Jennifer L. *Maladies of the Will: The American Novel and the Modernity Problem*. University of Chicago Press, 2022.

Fleissner, Jennifer L. "Wharton, Marriage, and the New Woman." In *The Cambridge History of the American Novel*, edited by Leonard Cassuto, Claire Virginia Eby, and Benjamin Reiss, 452–69. Cambridge University Press, 2011.

Fleissner, Jennifer L. *Women, Compulsion, Modernity: The Moment of American Naturalism*. University of Chicago Press, 2004.

Foote, Stephanie. *The Parvenu's Plot: Gender, Culture, and Class in the Age of Realism*. University of New Hampshire Press, 2014.

Fraiman, Susan. *Unbecoming Women: British Women Writers and the Novel of Development*. Columbia University Press, 1993.

Gagnier, Regenia. *The Insatiability of Human Wants: Economics and Aesthetics in Market Society*. University of Chicago Press, 2000.

Gerber, Philip. Introduction to *Trilogy of Desire: Three Novels by Theodore Dreiser*. World Publishing, 1972.

Gilbert, Sandra M. "The Second Coming of Aphrodite." In *Kate Chopin*, edited by Harold Bloom, 89–113. Chelsea House Publishers, 1987.

Gilbert, Sandra M., and Susan Gubar. *No Man's Land: The Place of the Woman Writer in the Twentieth Century*. Vol. 2. Yale University Press, 1989.

Giorcelli, Cristina. "Edna's Wisdom: A Transitional and Numinous Merging." In *New Essays on The Awakening*, edited by Wendy Martin, 109–48. Cambridge University Press, 1988.

Glasgow, Ellen. *Barren Ground*. Harcourt, 1985.

Glasgow, Ellen. *A Certain Measure: An Interpretation of Prose Fiction*. Harcourt, 1943.

Glasgow, Ellen. *Phases of an Inferior Planet*. Harper, 1898.

Glasgow, Ellen. Preface to *Barren Ground*. Harcourt, 1985.

Glazener, Nancy. *Reading for Realism: The History of a U.S. Literary Institution, 1850–1910*. Duke University Press, 1997.

Grant, Robert. *Unleavened Bread*. Charles Scribner's Sons, 1900.

Hadley, Elaine. *Living Liberalism: Practical Citizenship in Mid-Victorian Britain*. University of Chicago Press, 2010.

Hardy, Thomas. Preface to *Tess of the d'Urbervilles*. Oxford University Press, 1988.

Hemingway, Ernest. *The Sun Also Rises*. Scribner, 2006.

Herrick, Robert. *One Woman's Life*. Macmillan, 1913.

Herrick, Robert. *Together*. Macmillan. 1908.

Hirsch, Marianne. "From Great Expectations to Lost Illusions: The Novel of Formation as Genre." *Genre* 12, no. 3 (1979): 293–311.

Howard, June. *Form and History in American Literary Naturalism*. University of North Carolina Press, 1985.

Howells, William Dean. *A Modern Instance*. Houghton Mifflin, 1909.

Howells, William Dean. *The Rise of Silas Lapham*. W. W. Norton, 1982.

James, Henry. *The American*. Charles Scribner's Sons, 1907.

James, Henry. *The American Scene*. In *Collected Travel Writings: Great Britain and America*, 351–736. Viking Press, 1993.

James, Henry. *Hawthorne*. Harper & Brothers, 1880.

James, Henry. Preface to *The Novels and Tales of Henry James: The American*, edited by Percy Lubbock. Charles Scribner's Sons, 1907.

James, Henry. "The Real Thing." In *The Tales of Henry James*, edited by Christof Wegelin and Jenry B. Wonham, 189–210. W. W. Norton, 2003.

James, William. "What Pragmatism Means." In *Pragmatism, Old and New: Selected Writings*, edited by Susan Hack, 289–308. Prometheus Books, 2006.

Jameson, Fredric. "Antinomies of the Realism-Modernism Debate." *Modern Language Quarterly* 73, no. 3 (2012): 475–85.

Jameson, Fredric. *Postmodernism, or, The Cultural Logic of Late Capitalism*. Duke University Press, 2001.

Kaplan, Amy. *The Anarchy of Empire in the Making of U.S. Culture*. Harvard University Press, 2005.

Kaplan, Amy. *The Social Construction of American Realism.* University of Chicago Press, 1992.

Kazin, Alfred. *On Native Grounds: An Interpretation of Modern American Prose.* Reynal & Hitchcock, 1942.

Koenigs, Thomas. *Founded in Fiction: The Uses of Fiction in the Early United States.* Princeton University Press, 2021.

Kouwenhoven, John. "What's 'American' about America?" In *The Jazz Cadence of American Culture,* edited by Robert O'Meally, 123–36. Columbia University Press, 1998.

Lant, Kathleen Margaret. "The Siren of Grand Isle: Adèle's Role in *The Awakening.*" In *Kate Chopin,* edited by Harold Bloom, 115–24. Chelsea House Publishers, 1987.

Leavis, F. R. *The Great Tradition.* New York University Press, 1960.

Levy, Helen Fiddyment. "Coming Home: Glasgow's Last Two Novels." In *Ellen Glasgow: New Perspectives,* edited by Dorothy Scura, 220–34. University of Tennessee Press.

Lewis, Pericles. *The Cambridge Introduction to Modernism.* Cambridge University Press, 2007.

Link, Eric Carl. *The Vast Terrible Drama: American Literary Naturalism in the Late Nineteenth Century.* University of Alabama Press, 2004.

Livingston, James. *Pragmatism, Feminism, and Democracy: Rethinking the Politics of American History.* Routledge, 2001.

Livingston, James. "War and the Intellectuals: Bourne, Dewey, and the Fate of Pragmatism." *The Journal of the Gilded Age and Progressive Era* 2, no. 4 (2010): 431–50.

Locke, John. *Two Treatises of Government.* Edited by Peter Laslett. Cambridge University Press, 2005.

Lukes, Steven. *Individualism.* Basil Blackwell, 1973.

MacIntyre, Alasdair C. *After Virtue: A Study in Moral Theory.* 2nd ed. University of Notre Dame Press, 1984.

Malcolm, Janet. "The Woman Who Hated Women." *The New York Times Book Review,* November 16, 1986.

Martin, Jay. *Harvests of Change: American Literature, 1865–1914.* Prentice-Hall, 1967.

Matthews, Pamela R. *Ellen Glasgow and a Woman's Traditions.* University Press of Virginia, 1994.

Maupassant, Guy de. "The Necklace." In *100 Great Short Stories,* edited by James Daley, 234–42. Dover, 2015.

McCullough, Kate. *Regions of Identity: The Construction of America in Women's Fiction, 1885–1914.* Stanford University Press, 1999.

McKeon, Michael. Introduction to *The Theory of the Novel: A Historical Approach,* edited by Michael McKeon, xiii–xviii. Johns Hopkins University Press, 2000.

Mead, George Herbert. "The Social Self." In *Pragmatism, Old and New: Se-lected Writings*, edited by Susan Hack, 477–85. Prometheus Books, 2006.

Melville, Herman. "Bartleby, the Scrivener: A Story of Wall-Street." In *Billy Budd and Other Stories*, edited by Frederick Busch, 1–46. Viking Penguin, 1986.

Mencken, H. L. "New Fiction," review of *Barren Ground*, by Ellen Glasgow. In *Ellen Glasgow: The Contemporary Reviews*, edited by Dorothy Scura, 259. Cambridge University Press, 1992.

Mendelman, Lisa. *Modern Sentimentalism: Affect, Irony, and Female Authorship in Interwar America*. Oxford University Press, 2019.

Michaels, Walter Benn. *The Gold Standard and the Logic of Naturalism*. University of California Press, 1987.

Mitchell, Lee Clark. *Determined Fictions: American Literary Naturalism*. Columbia University Press, 1989.

Moretti, Franco. *The Way of the World: The Bildungsroman in European Culture*. Translated by Albert Sbragia. Verso, 2007.

Murphy, Geraldine. "Romancing the Center: Cold War Politics and Classic American Literature." *Poetics Today* 9, no. 4 (1988): 737–47.

Nevius, Blake. *Robert Herrick: The Development of a Novelist*. University of California Press, 1962.

Norris, Frank. *A Man's Woman*. AMS Press, 1970.

Norris, Frank. *McTeague*. In *Frank Norris: Novels and Essays*, edited by Donald Pizer, 261–572. The Library of America, 1986.

Norris, Frank. *The Pit*. Robert Bentley, 1971.

Norris, Frank. "A Plea for Romantic Fiction." In *The Norton Anthology of American Literature*, edited by Nina Baym et al. 8th ed. W. W. Norton, 2013.

Ohmann, Richard. *Selling Culture: Magazines, Markets, and Class at the Turn of the Century*. Verso, 1996.

Parvalescu, Anca. "To Die Laughing and to Laugh at Dying: Revisiting *The Awakening*." *New Literary History* 36, no. 3 (2005): 477–95.

Pizer, Donald. *Realism and Naturalism in Nineteenth-Century American Literature*. Southern Illinois University Press, 1966.

Poe, Edgar Allan. "The Purloined Letter." In *Edgar Allan Poe: The Complete Stories*, 684–701. Knopf, 1992.

Rabaté, Jean-Michel. *1913: The Cradle of Modernism*. Blackwell, 2007.

Raper, Julius Rowan. "*Barren Ground* and the Transition to Southern Modernism." In *Ellen Glasgow: New Perspectives*, edited by Dorothy Scura, 146–61. University of Tennessee Press, 1995.

Redfield, Marc. *Phantom Formations: Aesthetic Ideology and the Bildungsroman*. Cornell University Press, 1996.

Review of *The Custom of the Country*, by Edith Wharton. *The Nation*. May 15, 1913.

Rich, Adrienne Cecile. *The Fact of a Doorframe: Poems Selected and New 1950–1984*. W. W. Norton, 2002.

Rohy, Valerie. *Impossible Women: Lesbian Figures and American Literature*. Cornell University Press, 2000.

Rosowski, Susan J. "The Novel of Awakening." In *The Voyage In: Fictions of Female Development*, edited by Elizabeth Abel, Marianne Hirsch, and Elizabeth Langland, 49–68. University Press of New England, 1983.

Rowlette, Robert. "Tarkington in Defense of Howells and Realism: A Recovered Letter." *Forum* 14, no. 3 (January 1973): 64.

Sandel, Michael J. *Justice: What's the Right Thing to Do?* 1st ed. Farrar, Straus and Giroux, 2009.

Schultz, Elizabeth. "Out of the Woods and into the World: A Study of Interracial Friendships between Women in the American Novels." In *Conjuring: Black Women, Fiction, and Literary Tradition*, edited by Marjorie Pryse and Hortense J. Spillers, 67–85. Indiana University Press, 1985.

Scura, Dorothy, ed. *Ellen Glasgow: The Contemporary Reviews*. Cambridge University Press, 1992.

Showalter, Elaine. "The Death of the Lady (Novelist): Wharton's *House of Mirth*." *Representations* 9 (1985): 133–49.

Showalter, Elaine. "Spragg: The Art of the Deal." In *The Cambridge Companion to Edith Wharton*, edited by Millicent Bell, 87–97. Cambridge University Press, 1995.

Showalter, Elaine. "Tradition and the Female Talent: *The Awakening* as a Solitary Book." In *New Essays on The Awakening*, edited by Wendy Martin, 33–57. Cambridge University Press, 1988.

Simmel, Georg. "The Metropolis and Mental Life." In *Georg Simmel on Individuality and Social Structure*, edited by Donald Levine, 324–39. University of Chicago Press, 1971.

Slaughter, Joseph. *Human Rights, Inc.: The World Novel, Narrative Form, and International Law*. 1st ed. Fordham University Press, 2007.

Smith, Carl S. "Dreiser's *Trilogy of Desire*: The Financier as Artist." *Canadian Review of American Studies* 7, no. 2 (1976): 151–62.

Smith-Rosenberg, Carroll. *Disorderly Conduct: Visions of Gender in Victorian America*. 1st ed. Knopf, 1985.

Sorkin, Adam. "'She Doesn't Last, Apparently': A Reconsideration of Booth Tarkington's *Alice Adams*." *American Literature* 49, no. 2 (1974): 182–99.

Sorokin, Pitirim. "American Millionaires and Multi-Millionaires: A Comparative Statistical Study." *Journal of Social Forces* 3, no. 4 (1925): 627–40.

Spilka, Mark. "The Death of Love in *The Sun Also Rises*." In *Ernest Hemingway's "The Sun Also Rises": A Casebook*, edited by Linda Wagner-Martin, 33–45. Oxford University Press, 2002.

Stasi, Paul. *The Persistence of Realism in Modernist Fiction*. Cambridge University Press, 2022.

Steiner, Wendy. "The Causes of Effect: Edith Wharton and the Economics of Ekphrasis." *Poetics Today* 10, no. 2 (1989): 279–97.

Steiner, Wendy. *The Real Real Thing: The Model in the Mirror of Art*. University of Chicago Press, 2010.

Strawson, Galen. "Against Narrativity." *Ratio* 17, no. 4 (2004): 428–52.

Strawson, Galen. *Locke on Personal Identity: Consciousness and Concernment*. Princeton University Press, 2014.

Strawson, Galen. "'We Live beyond Any Tale That We Happen to Enact.'" *Harvard Review of Philosophy* 18 (2012): 73–90.

Susman, Warren. *Culture as History: The Transformation of American Society in the Twentieth Century*. Pantheon, 1984.

Tarkington, Booth. *Alice Adams*. Doubleday, 1921.

Thayer, William Roscoe. "The New Story-Tellers and the Doom of Realism." In *Documents of American Realism and Naturalism*, edited by Donald Pizer, 159–66. Southern Illinois University Press, 1998.

Tompkins, Jane. *Sensational Designs: The Cultural Work of American Fiction, 1790–1860*. Oxford University Press, 1986.

Trachtenberg, Alan. *The Incorporation of America*. Hill and Wang, 1982.

Travis, Jennifer. "Accidents, Agency, and American Literary Naturalism." In *Cambridge History of American Women's Literature*, edited by Dale Bauer, 387–403. Cambridge University Press, 2012.

Wagner, Linda. *Ellen Glasgow: Beyond Convention*. University of Texas Press, 1982.

Waid, Candace. *Edith Wharton's Letters from the Underworld: Fictions of Women and Writing*. University of North Carolina Press, 1991.

Walker, Rafael. "James Weldon Johnson's Feminization of Biraciality." *Twentieth-Century Literature* 67, no. 4 (2021): 385–406.

Watt, Ian. *The Rise of the Novel: Studies in Defoe, Richardson and Fielding*. University of California Press, 1957.

Wharton, Edith. *A Backward Glance*. In *Edith Wharton: Novellas & Other Writings*, edited by Cynthia Griffin Wolff, 767–1064. The Library of America, 1990.

Wharton, Edith. *The Custom of the Country*. Penguin, 2006.

Wharton, Edith. "The Great American Novel." In Wegener, *Edith Wharton*, 151–59.

Wharton, Edith. *The House of Mirth*. W. W. Norton, 1994.

Wharton, Edith. "Permanent Values in Fiction." In *Edith Wharton: The Uncollected Writings*, edited by Frederick Wegener, 175–79. Princeton University Press, 1996.

Wharton, Edith. "Tendencies in Modern Fiction." In Wegener, *Edith Wharton*, 170–74.

Wharton, Edith. *The Writing of Fiction*. Touchstone, 1997.

Will, Barbara. "*The Great Gatsby* and the Obscene Word." *College Literature* 32, no. 4 (2005): 125–44.

Wolff, Cynthia Griffin. *A Feast of Words: The Triumph of Edith Wharton*. Oxford University Press, 1995.

Wolff, Cynthia Griffin. "Lily Bart and the Beautiful Death." *American Literature* 46 (1974): 16–40.

Wollstonecraft, Mary. *The Vindications of the Rights of Women*. In *The Vindications: The Rights of Men and the Rights of Women*, edited by D. L. Macdonald and Kathleen Scherf. Broadview Press, 1997.

Yaeger, Patricia S. "'A Language Which Nobody Understood': Emancipatory Strategies in *The Awakening*." *NOVEL: A Forum on Fiction* 20, no. 3 (1987): 197–219.

Zeitlin, Solomon. "The Time of the Passover Meal." *The Jewish Quarterly Review* 42, no. 1 (1951): 45–50.

Ziff, Larzer. "An Abyss of Inequality." In *Kate Chopin*, edited by Harold Bloom, 17–24. Chelsea House Publishers, 1987.

Zimmerman, David. *Panic! Markets, Crises, and Crowds in American Fiction*. University of North Carolina Press, 2006.

INDEX

www.ingramcontent.com/pod-product-compliance
Lightning Source LLC
Chambersburg PA
CBHW031558060326
40783CB00026B/4135